Letter to My Family

Letter to My Family

Janina Dreslius Zdanys

Grey Willow Press

Copyright © 2019 by Ramute Zdanys Mills, Jonas Zdanys, and Leonas Zdanys. Translated from the Lithuanian by Jonas Zdanys. All rights reserved.

ISBN 978-1-7338882-0-2

Cover design by Regina Schroeder / forgetgutenberg.com

Manufactured in the United States of America

Grey Willow Press
greywillowpress.org
greywillowpress@gmail.com

PART ONE

Lithuania
World War II
In the Camps

February 21, 2002

My dear ones –

I will begin to write the memories of my life.

Perhaps they won't be especially interesting, but I write so my children would know what the road of my life has been.

Though many years have already passed and I won't be able to remember everything, I will nonetheless begin with what I remember from my childhood, my youth, and so on.

I was born on the ninth day of December in the year one thousand nine hundred twenty-seven (12-9-1927), in Šančiai, a district of Kaunas.

My parents were Arturas Dreslius, my father, who was born February 10, 1902, in Plikalnis, not far from Kaunas, and my mother, Viktorija Župerkaitė, who was born July 10, 1893, in Dotnuva.

Mama worked in Kaunas and the two of them met each other there because Tėtis also worked in Kaunas. They were married on May 24, 1924. Though Mama was nine years older than Tėtis, they got along and lived together nicely. Tėtis had a job working in a linen factory and we lived in Panemunė, which was part of Kaunas. There, my brother Pranas was born, on May 7, 1925, and a year later, on September 12, 1926, my brother Povilas.

Life there wasn't bad. Mama knew how to sew, so she earned extra money for herself, making dresses and other clothes for children.

Though my father's family lived not too far away, my grandmother didn't like my mother. That was because my mother was a Catholic and my father was a Lutheran and, before their wedding, he had converted to Catholicism. In addition, Mama was much older, so they all were very much against that marriage. So Mama had many unpleasant interactions with them, but she accepted everything and never argued or fought with them.

After I was born, as Mama used to tell me, the linen factory burned down. Tėtis was left without a job and they had many difficulties because they had not saved any money. Mama sewed a lot but what she earned wasn't enough for everything. And then, on December 16, 1931, my brother Stasys was born. Tėtis tried to make ends meet by working many different jobs. He had a good head and good hands, never shied away from work, and did all he could to make sure that it would be a bit easier for us to live.

We lived in Panemunė near the Nemunas. Little remains in my memory of that time, but I do know that we bathed in the Nemunas and Mama dried our towels on nearby bushes, and there was a fence made of wood there and I used to sit on it. I was four years old then.

I remember when they took Mama to the hospital. We were standing next to her bed and Mama cried, saying that we should be good and she would bring us a little brother.

We were looked after by a woman we used to call Gramma. When Mama came home she put the little one into a cradle. He was so red.

Because there was so much unemployment at the time in Kaunas, my parents decided to go to Dotnuva, to stay with my mother's father. I remember traveling in a wagon and it was so dark. There was something like a tent stretched above the wagon.

When we arrived at my Grandpa's, Mama's sister Teklė was already living there with her children. There wasn't much room, so we children slept on blankets on the floor. It was summer and we spent most of our time outdoors. Grandpa didn't walk much, only with canes, because one of his legs was shriveled. In the evenings, outside or in the house, Grandpa told us many stories about his life. When he was young, he worked on an estate and the owner there was very mean and he beat my Grandpa if he didn't do what he was told to do exactly the way the owner wanted it done.

Mama's sister Mikalina also told us many stories. If someone in those days had written down her stories, it would have made a good book for children. It was good being there; we went to pick berries, hunt for mushrooms.

Grandpa couldn't walk well enough, and when he wanted to go to the cemetery to visit his wife's (our Grandma's) grave, we would help Grandpa into a small cart my cousin Jonas had and we young children would push him from behind and Jonas would be in front – like a horse, Grandpa would say – and we would drive him to the cemetery. It wasn't too far, maybe three-quarters of a kilometer. Jonas would take Grandpa onto his back when we got to the gates and would carry him to Grandma's grave. There was a bench there and he would sit until he wanted to go home again. There were many strawberries below the cemetery and we picked them, threaded them onto long stalks of grass, and gave them to Grandpa. And then the journey back. It was great entertainment. We rejoiced that Grandpa was so happy with that journey.

As Mama used to tell me about those days, it was a hard time, but we didn't notice. We spent our time outdoors. We had food to eat. We ran around in the yard even if we had no shoes.

Tėtis began to work at the Dotnuva Agricultural College, building a fence around the gardens. We children spent a great deal of time with him, my brothers already handing him what he needed. It wasn't far from Grandpa's house, maybe a kilometer. Tėtis was gifted, made many headstones because people asked to raise them in the cemetery. Tėtis made a granite headstone for Grandma's grave, which stands even today. (When we were in Lithuania, in 1989, we visited that grave. My Tėtis's handiwork still looked good.)

Tėtis worked many jobs to ensure that his family would be all right. But because we all lived together there, including my Aunt Teklė and her children, we all ate together and the food wasn't too plentiful. We children would walk over to the Agricultural College. There was a very beautiful park, a large pond filled with fish. We went to the cafeteria to ask for bread. After we ate, we would feed those fish. It was great fun to see whose bread the fish would take first. The park was very beautiful. The Count and Countess were buried there, and they left it all to the College. People would say that there was money buried there, but if you wanted to find it you had to dig for it only at night, but we were all afraid of that and we forfeited our chance to be rich.

When you start to think about your childhood you become saddened by so many little things. Even those years when we had such hardship today seem wonderful.

That's how the years passed. Though Grandpa was very good to us, Mama began to say that it would be good to have a place of our own. At the other end of Grandpa's double house lived my Mama's brother Antanas. He and his family controlled the orchard, the garden, and didn't give us anything. But we children took things anyway, without permission. The apples were delicious, though if they saw us they would shout at us, scolding us for picking unripe fruit. Once every two weeks they baked bread. There was a large oven, which they heated with wood. They mixed the dough in a tub, kneaded it, made loaves, and placing it onto a wooden peel they pressed into in a cross shape and baked it in the oven on the dried leaves of sweet flag or cabbage. That fresh bread smelled so wonderfully when they took it out baked and put it on the bench to cool. We children waited impatiently when we would be able to eat it. That's how we lived for a year and a half with Grandpa.

Tėtis received a telegram from his mother that Albert (Tėtis's brother) shot himself in the head and was lying in the hospital, that we should come to her. Tėtis said, well we have to go, shipped our things, and we took the train. At the station was waiting Tėtis's brother Rudolf and he hired a coach and we drove to Zuikinė, the Fifth Fort, where Grandma lived. It was already dark when we arrived. Grandma gave us bread and milk and made a bed for us in the corner. My brother Stasys and I slept together, he was a year-and-a-half old. We children didn't like our Grandma, we were afraid of her. She had little to do with us. We were given food and sat quietly with Mama.

The grownups all sat together to eat at the table, we children were given meals on a bench, but there was no place for Mama at the table. She had nothing to eat for three days. Tėtis thought that Mama was eating with the children. After three days, Mama couldn't stand it any longer and told Tėtis that she hadn't eaten. Tėtis became very angry and immediately began to look for somewhere else to live.

Albert had already recovered and had come home. So there was not much room. After a day, Tėtis got one room in the house of Bauža in Zuikinė. There wasn't much room there. There were six of us and we children slept on a bench. There was my parents' bed and a few boxes, and that was all of my parents' wealth.

Tėtis began to look for work but couldn't find any because we weren't registered in Kaunas. We hadn't lived there for a year-and-a-half so there was no aid or assistance available. It was difficult to live, it was hard with food. We wanted to eat but there was nothing. Mama went to the priest to ask for help. He gave her a couple of *litai* and she brought back two loaves of bread. We children were so happy that we had bread. It was winter and I so wanted to go on the sled down the hill but I had nothing to wear. I took Mama's scarf and wrapped myself up in it and stepped into Mama's galoshes and slid down the hill.

I remember how Tėtis would go looking for work. It was still dark when he got up and left to walk to Kaunas on foot, about seven kilometers. He'd get some little job, earn a couple of *litai*, and would bring home bread. If Mama would cook some sort of soup without meat, we would then eat. When there was nothing at all to eat, Tėtis would go to his mother asking for something. She'd give him some sort of loaf of bread. Tėtis said he'd go get some potatoes somewhere. In those days, there was this fashion where people would dig holes in the field and pour potatoes into them to keep for the winter. Tėtis went to his mother's hole and filled a sack with potatoes but said he couldn't lift it. It was hard for him, so he poured half those potatoes back and climbed out with half a bag. He carried it home on his shoulders, and though it wasn't far it was difficult because he had so little strength then, not having eaten properly for so long. We children ate those potatoes with fermented cabbage, and it was so delicious. Tėtis's brother Rudolf would come visit us and would bring bread. We didn't need a lot, bread alone was also delicious. That woman in whose house we lived was good to us and we got this and that from her as well sometimes.

Mama got sick. She was cleaning the hospital's windows because that's the job she found and it turns out she was pregnant, four months, as she would tell me. She began to bleed that night. She stayed at home for a few days because there was no hospital nearby, and then she started to run a fever, got sicker and sicker. Tėtis borrowed a horse and wagon from one of the neighbors, lined the back of the wagon with bedding, and layed Mama down. We were crying, and Mama already didn't recognize us. I remember that very clearly. Tėtis drive the wagon to the Red Cross Hospital in Kaunas. How difficult it was for him, because he had no money and they would not admit her into the hospital. Because Tėtis had been a volunteer in the army, and because the chief of police knew him well since they had served together in the army, the chief called the hospital and told them to admit mama immediately. Mama had been left outside with a high fever. By the time Tėtis had run around everywhere trying to take care of this, Mama was lying in the corridor because people passing by saw that she was hemorrhaging and was sitting delirious with fever on the hospital's outside steps. They demanded that the woman, who they said would die if not taken in, be brought into the hospital. Orderlies came and placed her down in the corridor. Mama was later admitted and taken to a room. She was very ill and was in the hospital for six weeks with a blood infection.

Tėtis went to the hospital and pleaded with them to help her since she did not recognize anyone. An old doctor came in and told Tėtis that he would try to do what he could, whatever could still be done. He found some medicine which did bring Mama back to us, and after six weeks she came home. When Tėtis visited Mama, he was given rolls to take back to us children. Some of the nurses were very good to us.

When Mama was taken to the hospital, from Dotnuva arrived my Mama's sister Mikalina, to look after us. She was a spinster, with no patience, and used to hit us. But what could we do, Tėtis still had no steady job and went each day to try to find whatever work he could and we needed to be looked after. There was so little space, the room was small, and we were four children. We got stomachaches often, from the food, and we had to go to the outhouse to take care of our business. We were afraid to go by ourselves so Tėtis had to go with us. We children were so happy when Mama came home. It was in the spring. Just as Mama arrived, Mikalina went home. We were so happy she wasn't there. Though Mama was still weak, she did our laundry and looked after us.

Because there was so little room there, Tėtis said that we would be moving to Panemunė. He said it might be better there and he wouldn't have to walk through the woods to get to Kaunas to look for work. So we moved to Panemunė (part of Kaunas). Tėtis found an apartment with two rooms. It was an old house but we rejoiced that we had our own place. I remember there was a yard there and we sat on the grass.

There was an old man named Tamošius there and he would bring us bagels. Tėtis still kept looking for work and went to Petrašiūnai, across the Nemunas from Panemunė, where the paper mill was. He went to the mill to look for work and, walking through the factory, met his former boss from the linen factory. He was now the head of the paper mill. Tėtis immediately got a job there. He returned to Panemunė so happy that he had bumped into Bonikempfer (he was of German descent) there and with whom Tėtis had been in good stead at the linen factory.

He immediately said we would move to Petrašiūnai. Well, it was once again a new place for us children. I remember how Tėtis moved his things across the Nemunas. Before that he had gotten an apartment with a couple of rooms in a house owned by Astrauskas, right on the banks of the Nemunas, a very beautiful place. We were so happy that we would once again be able to swim in the Nemunas. Not far away were the Pažaislis Woods. The mistress of the house was a tailor, she had a great deal of work, so Mama would help her out and earned a few *litai*. They had a cow, so she brought milk for us, too.

Tėtis had a steady job in the factory and was paid every two weeks. There was no longer as much hardship. The Astrauskas children were older than we were, so we went out with them in row boats on the river. In the middle of the Nemunas was an island with lots of red and black currants. We picked them and Mama cooked currant preserves for us, which we ate with pancakes. I played dolls with their daughter, whose name was Janė. We sewed dresses for them and we each had our own dolls. Mine was sewn together out of cloth, but I was happy that I had a doll of my own.

After a time we found an apartment not far from the factory. The school was nearby. That's how my road to an education began. I walked to school with a friend of mine, her name was Onutė. The school was in a regular house, one large room. The teacher was good, was already elderly, her last name was Montvilienė. She taught me from first grade until my third year. I started school when I was seven years old, in 1934.

They started construction on a new school near us. Everyone was happy because it would be large and new. We found a different apartment, on the second floor of a house owned by a man named Ambrazas, and I still have a photograph of that house. We had three rooms plus a kitchen. School wasn't far away and it was pleasant to walk there with my friends. Across the street from where we lived was an empty square, and every summer a circus came there. How we waited for them to arrive! Twice, the circus midget and his wife stayed with us. We were very interested that they were so small. They always gave us free tickets to go to the circus. It was wonderful, with much laughter at the things they did.

On Sundays we all went to church together. Once, Pranas and Stasys went fishing in the Nemunas on Sunday, and when Pranas cast his line and Stasys was standing farther behind him, Pranas' hook caught Stasys under his eyelid. What fear there was! They ran home together from the Nemunas. We had just come back from church. There was no hospital in Petrašiūnai, so it was good that a doctor lived in the house next door. He examined Stasys, bandaged his eye, and said he would take Stasys to the hospital in Kaunas because it wasn't possible for him to remove the hook. He had a car, so Mama and Tėtis went with him. We waited for them to come back and later, in the afternoon, Stasys returned with a bandaged eye (he was six years old). Mama said it wasn't good to go fishing on a Sunday. God punished them.

That's how the years passed.

Tėtis began to play in the factory orchestra. We were so bored as he sat in the house blowing his horn. Later they rented a small hall and all of them went there to practice. It was beautiful, all of them in their military uniforms. They played in parades, at funerals, and once they played on Kaunas Radio. We listened at home on the radio. Many times they played during the summer at the Pažaislis picnic. We children had a wonderful time. We had our group and we danced. After the picnic we walked home, all of the children, straight through the woods. We weren't afraid at all.

We moved to that house where that small hall was. Mama cleaned it, so we lived there for free. We lived pretty well. Tėtis got paid every two weeks so we had enough to eat and we had clothes. Mama made a lot of our clothes. When Tėtis's family sold a parcel of land in Zuikinė, Tėtis took his share and bought Mama a sewing machine. He also bought some new clothes for us. I was so happy! He bought me a coat that had a small fur collar, and it was my pride and joy.

In the sunmmer, when Tėtis had vacation, he went to a farmer he knew well and helped him put new roofs on the cottages and barns. Others asked Tėtis to help them, too, so he earned a fair amount of money. That farmer planted potatoes for us, and raised a pig, so we had meat of our own and we no longer had food shortages.

I went with Mama to her father's house for a few weeks each summer. My cousins were also more grown, so we spent a lot of time there, where we had run when we were little in the Agricultural College's gardens and fields. Grandpa was by then not feeling well and mostly sat in the yard.

It's lovely to remember my childhood, which, though it was poor, was pleasant. Because my cousins Elena and Onutė worked at the Agricultural College, we spent a lot of time in the hothouses. It was interesting to see how they grew vegetables. I especially liked tomatoes. They were so big. There's nothing more delicious than eating tomatoes on bread outside. My cousin Marytė was in charge of the cafeteria, so we used to eat there together with the students and, taking extra bread, went to the pond to feed the fish. It was wonderful to sit outside in the evenings. Because the house wasn't far from the railroad tracks, trains would fly by just past the yard. It was the kind of time that passes quickly and we then returned home.

When Tėtis started to work in the factory, we got health insurance. Every summer, for six weeks, the insurance sent children to stay with wealthy farmers for vacation. The first time, we went to Vičiūnai, a village about twenty kilometers from us. We went – Povilas, Pranas, and I. Stasys was too young. That farm was in a beautiful place, near a lake. Four of us girls slept in one room, the boys were at the other end of the house. The food was very good. We ate five tines a day. As much milk as we wanted. It was good.

In the fall we went to the new school. It was big, made of brick, with large windows, two auditoriums. The school's opening was very impressive. I loved to read and couldn't wait until I could take books from the library. We could start taking books from the age of twelve. They had plays there, for Christmas. I had the chance to act several time as well. Because we lived near the Nemunas, many went to skate on the ice there. The Nemunas would freeze over before Christmas and all winter long there was thick ice. Even though we didn't have store bought skates, children managed to make their own. The banks were steep in places and it was fun to slide down and spin around on the ice on sleds.

In the spring, when it got warmer, the ice began to pop and crack and the Nemunas began to move. Many people went to watch how the ice flowed. It was beautiful and terrifying. The ice would get blocked up near Kaunas and the river would flood the meadows and fields. On Pentecost, the priest would bless the water, would say that no one could swim until the water was sanctified, but children would mostly not wait for that, we went swimming anyway.

I used to wait for summer vacation. Until we had to go somewhere, I walked with my friend to the woods and we would stretch out on the mosses there. How beautiful it was to look at the pine trees and listen to how they rustled. And how fragrant they were! Just outside the woods we would pick violets, blue and white. They were the most beautiful blossoms of spring.

And then I'd go again with Mama to Dotnuva for a few weeks. We'd spend the time there well. My cousin Marytė still worked in the cafeteria. I stayed with her and she took me all over the College. It was very interesting for me. I also went to visit my other cousins, Elena and Onutė. They worked in the hothouses.

Grandpa was quite sick. He mostly stayed in his bed. Mama would bring him food to eat. I was at Marytė's when my cousin Jonas came and told us that Grandpa had died. When I got back, he was already washed and laid out on a board. They dressed him in the the best of what he had, candles all around, and because it was summer people brought flowers from their gardens as well. Tėtis and my Aunt Paulina came from Kaunas. He was laid out in the room for two days. People sat around the table, sang hymns, ate, and sang again. I stayed with Marytė. His funeral was on the third day. He was taken by wagon to the Dotnuva church. After the mass, the priest came to the cemetery and buried Grandpa. Before we left, we came to say good-bye to Grandpa. We sat on that bench for a while. We went home.

That was in the summer of 1938. In mid-July we left again to summer for six weeks. This time they brought us to Lapės, a small town not far from Kaunas. We lived in a school. We older girls had our own room and the younger ones slept in a different room. There was a forest nearby and each day we went there. Our school was on a hill and at the foot of the hill flowed the river Nėris. We swam every day in the river, and after lunch – to the woods. There were many wonderful days there. My parents would come to visit and left me a little bit of money. There was a small store and we bought candy. Stasys was with me, so I gave him some as well. There was a church nearby. The pastor was old and had a large garden, so we went there to pick gooseberries and currants. It was very pleasant to sit on the banks and watch how boats passed by on the Nėris. Those six weeks passed quickly and I had to go home again. But at home it was pleasant, too, to spend time by the Nemunas.

In autumn it was back to school. Mama was a good woman. Though my grandmother didn't like her, Mama took care of her. She would buy her butter, sugar, preserves, and so on, and we children would have to bring those to her. Because Zuikinė was upcurrent on the Nemunas, Pranas would borrow a rowboat from Astraukas and he would row against the current, crossing over to the other side of the Nemunas, and Povilas and Pranas would take the basket and they'd both carry it. Grandma would take everything, would say that my Mama was kissing up to her, and that's why she was buying so much. She would give us pears and apples to eat and we, after visiting, would return home.

It's wonderful to float on the water. You sit and the water carries you. Pranas always steered the boat and we returned safe and sound. We would tell Mama that Grandma had said thank you, even though that wasn't true. No one from Tėtis's side ever visited us, as if we were not related. When Grandma received packages from America – her two sisters lived in Racine, Wisconsin – all of her children would come over and she would give each of them even a little something. She never gave anything to my father. But Tėtis never said anything. Mama was good, she helped Grandma a lot. If she got sick, Mama always went there to help her.

That's how the autumn passed, the winter. Everything seemed all right. Tėtis worked, we children went to school, Mama took care of the house. But there were many unpleasant things in my parents' lives. Mama told me many things when I became a teenager. Tėtis was a good father to the family, there was always something to eat, but his personal life wasn't always pleasant for Mama. Sometimes I'd see Mama crying and I would ask her what the matter was, but she would never say that there was anything unpleasant in her life. She would say – something heavy came upon my heart, so that's why I'm crying. At the time you could say that I was still a child. Tėtis belonged to the National Guard Veterans organization, had a uniform, looked very handsome, played in the horn ensemble. He went to various meetings, came home late. But that wasn't very often. I would hear how Mama would argue with my father. But I couldn't understand everything that was going on. I know that more than one woman circled around him. But he was good to us, was always working and was a good husband to Mama. What she wanted, he bought when there was money.

Mama's sisters often came to visit from Dotnuva. They'd each stay with us for a week. When they were going back home, Mama would buy them all sorts of things. She would fill baskets with food. I would wait impatiently for my cousin Marytė. (She is the mother of Ričardas.) She spent a few weeks with us every summer. We'd go to the Nemunas, would lie in the sun, swim, go for walks in the woods. My best vacations were with her. We'd go to the library. She paid 5 *litai* so I could take out books. That was my very best gift. I couldn't take out all of the books, but those that fit my age I read them all. But I was most interested in everything that was written about America. I read everything I could find. I never imagined that I would ever live in that storied land.

Autumn came again with its beauty. School again and all kinds of activities. During free time in winter we skated on the ice. Because winters were cold and there was a lot of snow, streets weren't plowed because they had no such equipment, and the sidewalks weren't cleared, so it was necessary to walk to school through the snow, and that was so much fun and we often came home wet because we were pushed into the snow. At last I received a pair of ice skates for Christmas. It was the greatest gift to me. My friends also had skates, so we spent a lot of time together on weekends and during Christmas break on the Nemunas. In the winter we brought filled baskets to Grandma in Zuikinė on a sled many times and we returned home late. Even though it was late, the evenings weren't so dark, the snow was white, and we weren't afraid.

In the school auditorium, from time to time, they held dances. Tėtis played, so it was free for us, we didn't have to pay an entrance fee. That's how my friend Valė and I began to learn to dance. The first man who led me out to dance was Polivas Borosevičius. He was the handsomest and the best dancer in all of Petrašiūnai. Though I was only twelve years old, I felt myself to be grown up and happy that I was already dancing. And how my friends envied me! I'll never forget this very pleasant moment of my youth.

They staged plays in the auditorium as well, and actors came with plays from Kaunas. The first time I went with Mama. The play was the classic comedy „America in the Sauna." I liked it very much. I remember even now how one woman in the play, a young woman, wanted to go to America, and how, after many intrigues, they locked her in a sauna when it was time to go and she never went to America.

During the winter, the school organized trips to museums and twice took children to the theater in Kaunas. I saw „Eglė, Queen of the Serpents," twelve brothers flying like blackbirds – How wonderful it was. I'll never forget that time. I liked „Hansel and Gretel" very much. I've never liked witches since then.

In the spring we went to visit Aunt Paulina (Mama's sister). She lived in Kaunas, not far from the Zoological Gardens, so we went to look around there, too. There was a movie theater nearby and I really liked Tarzan movies. I'll never forget how happy I was when I saw the German movie „Pearl of the East." Aunt Paulina was my godmother and I spent time frequently with her. Jonas, her son, was five years younger than I was. She bought us ice cream and we ate it together. Uncle Juozas drank too much and once told me to leave and go home, but it was already evening and it was seven kilometers for me. I didn't want to go but my aunt said she would walk with me for a bit. So off I went, alone, through the oak grove, and came home in the middle of the night. Mama was very concerned that I came home. But in those days it wasn't terrifying, because there weren't as many horrifying things happening as there are now.

The first time we went to the Valley of Song (Dainų slėnis) in Kaunas there was a song festival taking place. I went with my friend Valė and my brothers. There were many people there, so we two ended up alone and couldn't find my brothers. The festival ended past the middle of night. My brothers thought that we had already left. So the two of us struck out on our own for home. It was seven kilometers. We didn't encounter anyone, just when we arrived in our town some drunken men started to chase us, but the two of us were still quick and ran home. They couldn't keep up because we were fast and they were drunk. We returned safely.

In the summer we went to Mama's homestead again, and the time passed nicely there. When we returned in July, I went back to Lapės once more for six weeks. This time I went alone. We weren't little anymore. We had to act in a play and engage in a variety of other activities. I still have a photograph from that time. It was my last summer vacation in Lapės. At home I spent a lot of time by the Nemunas. Because it wasn't far from the Pažaislis Woods, many people came from Kaunas for the weekends. There were scout camps, and though I was not a girl scout I did spend much time in the camp.

In the fall I went mushrooming in the forest with Mama. There were many mushrooms and I knew them all. It was wonderful in the forest in the early morning. Mama would pack a lunch of bread and sausage, so we'd sit togther and eat it. You needed to have a license to pick mushrooms, and if the gamekeeper did come by, Mama knew him and he wouldn't say anything to us. Mama would pickle mushrooms and we had them through the winter. We went as well to the Pažaislis Church, which is very beautiful, in the Gothic style. They say that the painting hanging in the church was miraculous. It is Mary with the Infant. It was always covered with a green curtain, but during Mass they would open that covering. We also went to visit the cemetery of the Sisters of St. Casimir. The sisters lived at Pažaislis. There was a convent, a school, and they had a large orchard where we could buy apples. Mama would buy them by the bag and we children would bring them home in a small wagon. We had apple sauce all through winter.

Because we lived outside of Kaunas, my parents eventually had and kept pigs and rabbits. So we had meat during the winter as well. They planted potatoes in the spring and vegetables. In the fall they filled barrels with cabbage, pickles, beets. Tėtis had made a kind of cellar where they kept potatoes, cabbages, and cucumbers. We had our own vegetables all winter.

We lived in a small apartment. The kitchen was big, then one other room and one more small one. There was a bed in the kitchen and Pranas and Povilas slept there. In the larger room was my bed in the corner and Stasys' small bed. But during the day my bed converted to something like a bench and I used to sit on it. My parents slept in the small room, which now seems to me to have been no bigger than a good sized closet. But there was enough room for us all.

Tėtis made a sofa that looked as if it had been bought in a store. We had a radio. Every Sunday there was a program called „Children's Corner" so some of our friends came to listen as well. For Christmas my parents decorated a tree, and though it wasn't big it had beautiful ornaments on it and Mama would also hang candies and apples on it.

That's how winter would pass and I believed everything was good. Though my parents worried that we would have enough to eat, that we would have clothes. Tėtis worked in the paper mill so he was able to buy this material they called „filcas" – a rectangular sheet of wool. So Mama used to sew coats for us, pants; it was good wool material, so it could be unraveled and Mama also had thread so she knit socks and gloves for us.

In that building where we lived, on the second floor, was a large room, like an auditorium, and the paper mill's orchestra used to rehearse there. Mama, as I said, cleaned that room so our apartment was free for us. In addition, Pranas cleaned the horns for those who wanted their instruments cleaned, so he got a *litas* or so. When they held dances in that hall, Pranas used to play the drums, and he was very happy that he was able to participate in that orchestra.

That's how the spring of 1940 arrived. Something was not all that right. Neighbors often came over and they all listened to the news on the radio. I already knew that a year earlier the Germans had started to attack and grab other countries. People were very worried about what would happen to us. Word spread that the Russians were coming to Lithuania. When the Russians were helping the Germans in 1939 when they were attacking Poland, the Russians took Vilnius – which the Poles had taken from us – away from the Poles and returned it to Lithuania. I remember the celebrations when our Lithuanian army marched into Vilnius. Everyone rejoiced that, at last, Vilnius was once again our capital. Others said, don't celebrate too much because it could be that Vilnius is ours and we are the Russians'. And that's how it was. And in June the Russian army marched into Lithuania.

It was interesting for us to watch how Russian tanks, trucks, drove down the road, and how we and many other people sat on the banks of the Nemunas and some Russian officer looked at maps but couldn't figure them out and asked us in which direction was Kaunas. How exhausted their soldiers looked, how dirty. And how they all looked at us. Though the Jews greeted them like some kind of heroes and threw flowers at them, they did not smile. How quickly everything changed. Red flags appeared everywhere, there were meetings, speeches, and they all cursed the government of Smetona. Because just as the Russians were crossing the Lithuanian border, our president Antanas Smetona crossed the border into Germany – he escaped. Schools immediately hung Stalin's portrait and all of us students had to worship him. They immediately began to teach the Russian language. Movie theatres showed Russian films. There were many things that we children liked, because we had never before seen such big meetings. They forced students to go and to shout during those meetings that now „everything was better."

There were many Russians and they were everywhere. Sitting on the sidewalks, they played their harmonicas and danced their dances, which we had not seen before. In the evenings, when it was already dark, they made a screen out of a bedsheet and showed films for children, and we all went to watch. The Russians and their followers always kept saying that now life would be better, that now it was the government of the workers and there would be no more masters. And we children believed that. Pranas worked in the glass factory. When the Russians came they put this woman into the former director's place, and she could not read or write. In a position in which she had to run the entire factory, she understood and knew nothing. Many of those who were supporters of communism got good positions, while educated people were left without jobs.

Tėtis worked in the paper mill. He was required to go to all sorts of gatherings to listen to speeches about how it would all be so much better now. And if you didn't go, you were their enemy. Tėtis had been a member of the Veterans' Organization, which the new government did not like, and he fell into difficulty. The newspaper published a story that Tėtis was a bad worker, that he agitated others not to work, that he was a drunkard, and so on. Tėtis had so many difficulties because of that. He had to hire a lawyer and it took several months until he could prove that those accusations weren't true. The newspaper eventually retracted those statements, said that they weren't true and apologized, but the damage had already been done.

That summer, Tėtis's brother Albertas came and said that we should all go to Germany. At that time, the German government accepted everyone who was even partly of German ancestry and invited all to come live in Germany. We children didn't want to move to a foreign country because we didn't know the language, and how could we leave our friends and that land we had loved since childhood. We didn't want to know anythng about that. Mama also didn't want to go, because her sisters were here, her friends. What could Tėtis do, if his family wouldn't go?

Things started to get worse. Already in the stores we couldn't buy many things because the Russians were buying up so much that there was nothing good left. And they began to fire people from their jobs. If you were an engineer, get out, and they put someone in your place who didn't know anything. Tėtis was pushed to work outside with the logs. In his place they put some other person. They disbanded the veterans' group. They changed the police to the militia. Tėtis's friends would come over and would say to him that it would be better if he ran from here. Tėtis's brothers said that they all would leave and why would he stay by himself, he'd be deported to Siberia. But what could Tėtis do if his family said they would not leave?

That's how the summer passed, the autumn. In December, Mama and I went to visit Tėtis's sister Greta, who lived near the Latvian border. We traveled by train, stopped for a visit in Dotnuva, saw Mama's sister, and late in the evening we arrived near the border with Latvia. My uncle had been a border policeman but he was told that he was being relieved of his duties. He said that he and Aunt Greta would not be there for long and that they would be leaving to live with his parents in Mosėdis. The time there passed very nicely. My uncle showed me the border, we went to a store on the Latvian side, and having stayed there for a week, Mama and I returned home.

When we got home, we found much that was not right. Tėtis said that we would need to go to Germany. We cried, but there was nothing we could do. The Russians were threatening Tėtis, neighbors told him that Russians had come looking for him, and he said that he managed to avoid them one night by jumping out the back window of our apartment. He was afraid they would take us all.

That Christmas we children decorated the tree. I remember how Russian soldiers came then and asked us what that was, why did we need such a thing. When the radio was playing Christmas music, they commanded us to change the station to Moscow, where Russian music was playing. We couldn't say anything to them, they did what they wanted.

On the second day of Christmas, Tėtis's brother Albertas came to see us. He brought some sort of papers, various documents, so Tėtis could prove that he had descended from a German family. So he began right after Christmas to make all the necessary arrangements and to prepare for the journey. They nailed together wooden boxes, butchered a pig and salted the meat, said we would be bringing it to Germany. They took care of all the papers and then German soldiers came to our apartment. They looked so big, so tall, their uniforms were handsome, they smoked cigars. They said that we children would be taken care of there. Mama began to buy everything for us, clothing, shoes, and so on. Mama's sisters arrived and took everything they could, sold the furniture, and we slept the last night on the floor because there were no beds.

That's how February 8, 1941, arrived. My parents' friend arrived with a wagon and at four in the morning we left for Kaunas. The train station. I will never forget how difficult it was to leave everything that was dear to me, school, my friends, and those places that were so loved when seen through the eyes of a child. I was in the sixth grade, in the fall I would have been in the third class of grammar school, but everything changed. We were sitting in the wagon, and today I still see those lights when we got to the top of the hill and everything sank into darkness and I looked back. And I was so sad. Everything stayed behind and I was moving toward a distant land whose language I didn't even know. I saw how Mama wiped her eyes with her handkerchief; perhaps she, too, was weeping that we were leaving our homeland.

We arrived at the train station. It was still dark, cold. The train was standing there but they did not let us board. We went to the waiting room, and oh how I wanted to stay for a little while somewhere warm. More people began to arrive. Our boxes were stacked on the platform. Mama had, in a basket, bread and sausage. She got some tea in the station cafeteria so we ate breakfast. Finally, at around ten o'clock, they allowed boxes to be loaded onto the train car. Before twelve, they let everyone into the cars. But before that they examined papers so thoroughly that we thought we wouldn't be able to leave. Tėtis had to open all of our boxes and suitcases. The Russians unpacked everything we owned, removed and threw away the photographs my old teacher had given me so I would have remembrances.

When we climbed into the train car I stretched out on the bench and fell alseep. Mama shook me awake and said we're leaving now. We passed through Kaunas, the train flew through the fields. It was so sad that we now would never return. The train stopped at the Kybartai station. It was already dark. I wanted so much to eat, but most of all to drink something. Tėtis took a bottle and wanted to go to the station to get some water or tea, but when the door was opened a Russian immediately pointed a rifle at him and told him to go back. Tėtis said a Russian almost shot him. So he scraped a few handfuls of snow off the roof of the train car and we ate it. The train stood in the station for a few hours and the Russians again checked our papers. They behaved very rudely with us. They asked my brother Pranas if he would like to stay. They said they would train him to be a *politruk*. My brother said, my parents are going so I'm going with them, too.

The train finally moved, slowly crossed the border, and we ended up in Eitkūnai, on the German side. In the station there looked to be a different world. A children's orchestra was playing, there were many soldiers, nurses, all of them very pleasant. They told us politely to step out. They led everyone to the station's cafeteria, where there were long tables with white tablecloths. And they gave us so much food that we could't eat it all, even though we were very hungry. There was as much tea as we wanted. And they gave us all kinds of sweets. So it was a party for us. They talked to us in German,m but we didn't understand what they were saying. Speeches were given, they welcomed all of us new arrivals. And then, finally, we climbed back into the train cars. And they gave us a basket with sandwiches, some oranges, a large thermos of tea, so we would have something to eat because they told us we would be traveling all night. There was a lot of room so we were able to sleep. It was pleasant to sleep. The train rocked us.

When it began to grow light, at around seven in the morning, we arrived in Ilowa, not far from Soltau, in eastern Germany. The train stopped and they began unloading all of our belongings. Some men arrived with a carriage and they began to take us and our baggage to the town. Ilowa is a small town. Earlier, it had been part of Poland, but now the Germans had taken it over. It was very cold and we were waiting impatiently until we could get a bed. We traveled about ten kilometers until we reached a house. Earlier, it had been a residence for Polish soldiers and they gave us a room. It was the first time I had seen bunk beds. There wasn't much room and we stacked our baggage in another room. The beds had mattresses, so Mama took out her own sheets, made the beds for us, and we were so tired that we fell quickly to sleep.

In the morning, Tėtis went to the cafeteria to get sandwiches and coffee. It was about a kilometer away. That's where we went to eat lunch and dinner. They let us rest there for a week. Because it was February, it was still cold and we couldn't go anywhere. It got boring just to sit in that room. Many around us were speaking in Polish. Mama and we children understood and, whenever there was an opportunity, we talked to the other children in Polish. None of them liked us, at first thinking that we were Germans. But when we were able to talk to each other, it got better.

Mama started to want to cook her own food, and because we had some of our own meat, she got some cabbage fron the Poles and we all ate a good dinner. Everything would have been good, but one day some German officers came and yelled at us, ordering us not to talk to the Poles again. We couldn't speak German, so when they were speaking to us we thought it was pretty funny, but they were staring at us angrily. When we arrived there, there were more Lithuanians who also could not speak German. My friend Marytė also couldn't, so they opened a school and all of us had to go learn the language. Sometimes they gave the children oranges or candies. Stasys and I used to go get it, but whatever it was they asked us we didn't understand and so we didn't get anything. Tėtis would go get it for us.

In March, when it got a little warmer, we went to the forest. Tėtis was our leader. We did that until May. Once they told us there was to be a big meeting and everyone had to go. My parents went. Those who were Germans – both husband and wife – were given German citizenship. Those who weren't both German – Tėtis was of German ancestry but Mama wasn't – didn't get citizenship. They received a small piece of paper that indicated they could only live in Old Germany. Those who had citizenship were immediately sent to eastern

Germany, as they then called it, where the Germans had occupied Polish lands. But all of us were still living in Ilowa. We attended school, even though it wasn't pleasant, but when there was a Lithuanian teacher, it was all right. Mama cried often and wanted to return to Lithuania. There were many arguments and I was afraid that Mama would leave us. Tėtis did everything he could while Mama did nothing, didn't clean the rooms, just sat by the window and wept.

Women would come and talk to her, would tell her about their experiences, would go for walks with her. Eventually, Mama recovered, and we were happy that all would be good again.

In May we were told to pack up our things and that we would be taken deeper into Germany. Once again, on the train, they gave us something to eat and drink. We traveled all night. They brought us to Magdeburg. We were there for a few weeks and then had to pack up our things and leave again. They brought us to a town whose name I don't remember. There was a large room there, with many beds, bunk beds. The women began to look at the beds and saw that they were infested with bedbugs. No one went inside. Instead, they went to the chief commandante and told him that the people didn't want to be bitten by bedbugs and would not stay there. So once again we got in line to get onto the train to travel farther.

Eventually we arrived in Bad Blankenburg. There was again a large room with beds, but it was clean and we accommodated ouselves there. People began to ask when we would be given a permanent place to live. We ate in the cafeteria, took many walks in the hills. It was a very beautiful place. Finally, they began to send people to various cities and towns. We were assigned a place not far from the town of Arnstadt, in Thuringia. They took our things off the train, packed them onto a truck, and brought us to the small town of Rudisleben. Houses there were newly-built, three stories high. We were given an apartment on the third floor, beneath the roof. There were four rooms, a bathroom, and we were very happy that we at last had a place of our own.

That's how I began my life in Germany. July and August passed well. There was a brook nearby and I spent most of my time there. Tėtis, a few days after we arrived, began to work in the Makowerke factory and Pranas had to start work in the fall. Stasys and I began to go to school. I didn't want to go at all, since I couldn't speak the language, but it wasn't our decision and we had to go. There were other Lithuanians there as well, who also didn't know the language.

Well, the Germans don't like foreigners. They made fun of us because we didn't know their language, but a few months passed and I began to understand much of what was being said. It was the sixth year of school. Though the local children didn't accept us, we had friends of our own and weren't afraid of them. In fact, my brother Povilas had more than one fight with them.

Everything was on ration cards and they didn't give much. In the morning, we got two slices of bread and some margarine. Mama made lunch, and though there was no meat she made soup out of boiled bones. There were just enough potatoes. Mama would go to the shops and would buy whatever was available without ration cards.

That summer, in 1941, the Germans started a war with the Russians. Mama rejoiced that the Russians were no longer in Lithuania and that we would be going home. We children also wanted that. Well, what could Tėtis do? He went to the German authorities and told them he wanted to go back. When he returned home, Tėtis told us that they didn't even want to listen to him, said they told him he would be locked up in a concentration camp if he came back one more time. Mama suffered at that news.

Mama also had to go to work in the same factory where Tėtis was working. Winter passed and Mama decided she would go visit her sisters. She had no papers, no documents, no license to take the train, but she set off with another woman nonetheless. They had many difficulties but got to Lithuania successfully. She visited her sisters but it was clear that not everything was as it should have been.

It was much better for us when she returned. I went to school, but in the summer, when we had school vacation, I had to go to work in a factory – called Poltewerke, a munitions factory – near Arnstadt. They assigned me to an office where I served as a kind of messenger or errand girl, delivering papers from one place to another. I liked that job. Everyone could see that I was still a child – not yet quite fifteen years old – so they didn't push me very hard. I was also already able to converse fairly well in German.

I had to be at the factory from 7:30 a.m. until 6:30 p.m. Every day I got up before six and had to take the bus. I got lunch at the factory, and Mama packed a couple of slices of bread for me, so I had enough to eat. I waited eagerly for Sunday so I could sleep a little longer. Also, on Sundays, we went to the movies, where they showed films for children older than fourteen. We stopped afterwards at the cafe for ice cream, and those were our great joys on Sunday.

In the fall I went back to school, but when school ended I had to go back to that same factory job. So from 1:00 p.m. until 6:30 p.m. I was at work. I also had to do my homework, though they didn't assign much. The teacher was an older man. All he cared about was that everyone would be reading and writing on their own, and he mostly sat in his chair and stared out the window.

That's how it was all that winter. I was very tired of that, going to school and then to work every day. I waited for spring, so it wouldn't be so cold to walk since I didn't have many clothes and there was a lot of snow and it got bitterly cold.

When summer vacation came, it was better. Though I had to work, I liked what I did. I went from one building to another carrying messages and doing errands, and I didn't have to hurry. Everyone in the offices knew me, and on occasion someone would give me an apple. In the summer, Mama once again traveled to Lithuania and took Stasys with her, because he didn't want to be by himself. I also very much wanted to go but they wouldn't let me out of work. I felt as if I was in jail, because what they said I had to do. I had a friend, so at least on Sundays the two of us went to the movies.

Mama returned and brought back with her some bacon, ham, and bread. O how delicious it was! I got some letters from my friends in Lithuania, they asked me why I didn't come to visit them. But what could I have written if they were checking letters? I always wrote that everything was good and that I was very happy. But that wasn't true and I cried on more than one occasion. But I didn't want to create any problems for myself or for my parents.

In the fall, it was more of the same, to school and to work. I had already learned spoken German well and I was doing well in school. They were also teaching us to read and write in Gothic German. That wasn't easy because the written alphabet was quite different from the Latin. When I was still in Lithuania, after the Russians came, I had to study Russian. It was easy for me because I already knew Polish and those two languages aren't that different. The Russian alphabet also isn't easy, but during those six months I learned it well enough and could write letters in Russian to Mama's brother who lived in Russia.

The war was half way to its end and more and more airplanes started to fly over head. At first, they didn't fly to where we were, but later they flew past us and began to bomb cities. We lived not far from Arnstadt. It was not a large city. Most of the factories were where I worked and where Tėtis worked. I know that in that factory where I worked they were making ammunition. Many of the buildings were underground, and what they were doing there we were not allowed to know.

It used to be that after we laid down to sleep, a few hours later we would have to get up and dress and run down to the cellar, where there was a shelter, and we'd wait until the all clear signal was sounded. It was so cold to sit in that shelter in the winter. After the all clear, then it was back to bed. In the beginning, we had to go to the shelter only rarely, but later we'd have to get up a few times every night. We always thought that the British wouldn't bomb our small town. We most feared that they would hit the factories and we would all die. One night, it was already spring, British airplanes came and began dropping bombs on or town. They destroyed many houses, the train station, the park, and about half a kilometer from us they dropped many bombs into the fields. We all sat in the shelter believing that our end had come. But they didn't hit the factories. Our apartment windows shattered from the noise. I was terrified of the bombings. Later still, they began to fly in the daytime as well. They shot from the airplanes at trucks on the ground. Once I was walking as a plane was approaching. I ran and junmed into a ditch because it started shooting at cars.

There was a great deal of hardship, but I can't write all of it down. We managed to survive. They also destroyed our movie theater so there was nothing to watch since it was the only one in town. They bombed it to pieces.

Winter passed and spring came once again. I was told to go to a different factory, to work in the cafeteria. So after classes, I went to work, not far from my house. When summer vacation came, I had to work there from morning until evening. When necessary, I also worked in the kitchen to assist with the preparation of food. It wasn't so bad, since there was more food and the woman in charge was good.
Every morning I got breakfast, two slices of bread and a bit of sausage or cheese. When we served lunch, I mostly collected

the ration cards. There were three service windows, one for Germans, the second for Poles and the French, and the third for Russians. I was at the Poles' window, and they begged me not to take their ration cards because they could then get food twice. They knew that I spoke Polish. But I tried not to do that, so the German women employees wouldn't see. I tried to help the best I could, but I knew that if I was caught I would have been punished.

That fall, Povilas was conscripted into the army, even though he was only eighteen years old. But he said he would be better off in the army and not at the factory. Mama cried and we were all afraid that Povilas was being taken. It appeared that the war was not going well for the Germans, so they were taking everyone who was still at home.

Just before Christmas in 1944, Pranas was taken into the army, so just Stasys and I remained with our parents. After the holidays, new people arrived from Lithuania. They settled where we lived. I found myself a friend, Anelė. She was eight years older, but we liked each other very much. We would go to the movies and when her parents arrived, Mama had a friend in her mother as well.

More people continued to arrive from Lithuania, because the Russians were already back in Lithuania and the Germans were fighting them on their own land. There were many French, Poles, and Russians where we lived, and they all were anxiously waiting for the Americans to get here quickly. And on the first day of Easter we saw our first American soldiers. They set up a kitchen in the yard and cooked their own food. And how we Lithuanians went to talk to them, and there were, among those soldiers, some of Lithuanian heritage, so we had enough food for ourselves as well. And how all the Poles and Russians were no longer afraid. They went from village to village stealing pigs and chickens from the German farmers. They gave some to us as well and we were so fortunate to have something to eat.

But a few weeks later our good life came to an end. The Americans began to make sure there was order, because the Poles and Russians had looted so many stores and warehouses as revenge against the Germans. They posted guards and the amount of food we got began to dwindle. Mama began to sew suits and shirts for the Russians, with material they had stolen from stores, so they brought food in payment. Some material was left over for Mama, too.

And May came. There weren't many soldiers left in our town, so people began to worry about what was going to happen next. One day we saw Povilas standing in the yard with a bicycle. We rejoiced that he had returned safely home. He said that just as soon as the war had ended, he changed out of his uniform into civilian clothes, got a bicycle from some Germans, and rode home for six hundred kilometers. My friend Birutė, who had arrived from Lithuania just a few months earlier, really liked Povilas. They began to see each other.

A little while later, people began to talk that the Americans were giving Thuringia to the Russians. Everyone was quite worried about what to do so we wouldn't end up in Russian hands. Even though the Americans were right here, they weren't particularly concerned about us. They kept asking us why we just didn't go back to our own countries. They said that the Russians were their good friends and that they were good people. At that time, the Americans had no idea what communism was. When we told them what the Russians had done in Lithuania, how many people they had deported to Siberia, and that we would end up in Siberia if we went back now, we couldn't convince them.

My parents and other people thought that the Americans might hand us over to the Russians. A week later, they rounded up all the men – young, old – and herded them into a big orchard. Tėtis also wound up there. There were no tents and nowhere to sit or lie down. Everyone brought them whatever food they had. Tėtis was very worried about what would happen next. Guards patrolled and wouldn't let anyone approach. It was good that there happened to be an American-Lithuanian soldier there, so Mama cried and asked why the men were being held. After three days, they let the men go.

The Americans went to German homes and took wine and, drunk, came to look for women. They came into our yard. Birutė and Mama and I climbed up to the attic and climbed out a window onto the roof. But they didn't look for us and we sat there for a few hours until the danger subsided. But most of the Americans were good men and would bring us food. One of our friends had a harmonica, so he had to play while they danced with the German girls. And the girls were happy because they even got chocolate.

In the evenings, we didn't go anywhere because the Russians, French, and Poles did what they wanted, looted stores, took whatever they desired from the Germans. But after a few weeks they were forbidden to do so, and much of that stopped.

We learned, shortly after, that in Bavaria, near Wurzburg, there was a camp for refugee Lithuanians, that all Lithuanians were going there. My friend Anelė's brother went there to take a look around. When he came back he said let's all go there. Tėtis with another man hired a truck, we once again loaded up our things, though we left most of what we had behind, and took our clothes and only what was necessary. It was sad again to leave, since I had become accustomed to this place. Well, everyone else left so we left, too, for Wurzburg.

The trip wasn't bad, about five hours. Thuringia is a beautiful place. We eventually reached the railroad station. They unloaded our things and the truck left us there. We sat on our boxes and Tėtis asked where we should go now. The entire town was in ruins, though the streets were clean. We had to find which direction the camp lay in. My friend Anelė and her family left for the camps in Hanau. I got on my brother's bicycle and peddled down the streets looking for the camp. I came to some sort of park. Up ahead were the ruins of a church. The weather was so beautiful, it was so peaceful. Suddenly I heard organ music, someone was playing „Ave Maria." It was so moving and brought me to tears. Many other people also stopped to listen. I will never forget what I felt then.

I met a man and he asked me where I was going. He was a Ukrainian. I asked him where the camp was and he said it was in Wurzburg Zell.

I told my parents. Tėtis found a man who drove us to the camp. For three days before that we had stayed in a destroyed house. Mama cooked food on a firepit stove made of piled rocks. It was very uncomfortable as we tried to sleep on bricks as wind whistled through all the holes in the walls. There was no other place to lie down.

We arrived at the refugee camp and there were many people there, not just Lithuanians. We found some sort of a place to live in a garage. Tėtis found some boards and made a place on the ground for us to sleep. I was just happy that I didn't have to sleep outside. We got food in the kitchen. They gave only small portions but we didn't go hungry. We found some Lithuanians we knew there as well. Not far from the camp was a field a wild peas, so we all picked them and ate them and it was delicious.

A week later, Povilas went to Bamburg and brought Birutė back with him. Because this camp was a big one, they decided that it was necesary to bring Lithuanians to a different camp. Tėtis and some other men had to go there to clean up that place. When he came back, Tėtis said it was a bunch of wooden barracks and a few brick buildings in the middle of the fields near an airport. It was where the Germans had had their own military base.

And so we once again loaded our possessions onto a truck and it brought us to Seligenstadt, not far, about eighteen kilometers from Wurzburg. It didn't look too bad to me. It was near the train station, there were many trees. They gave us a good room. It was a large room for two families. They put up a divider and we began to live. They gave us food and we got soup from the dining hall. All the men cleaned the camp, built more barracks. They built a church in one large garage.

There wasn't much to do there for young people. The weather was good so we spent a lot of our time outside, sitting near the railroad tracks on a small embankment. We had a flag and Tėtis raised it on the chimney so whoever drove past would know that there were Lithuanians living here. A few weeks later, Birutė and I were sitting on the bank and a train with a Lithuanian flag rolled past. They saw our flag and began to wave. I didn't know that the man who would be my husband was among them.

A few days later, more Lithuanians arrived from Wurzburg and they unloaded them in the middle of the camp. Birutė and I went to take a look. A blond young man was standing there. But we kept walking. One of the barracks was empty, a large chamber, so on weekends dances were held there. There was no orchestra, but if someone played the harmonica and young people and others gathered together there, some of them danced. Mama wanted to dance but Tėtis wouldn't go. So she and I used to go to watch how the young people danced. I was sitting on a bench with Mama, and when the music started that blond young man asked me to dance. He danced well and that evening he danced with me the most. I liked dancing with him. Mama liked him very much and she kept saying that that „blondy" looks good. We lived in one room with the Gaidelevičius family. They were from Kybartai and they knew that „blondy's" family. But because I was still young, I had other friends as well.

My friend Anelė used to come visit from Hanau. We got along very well. She began to take a look at the men here, but because she was older she didn't manage to find a boyfriend for herself. When Povilas started to date Birutė, she wanted to get married as quickly as possible. Though my parents told him to wait, said that Povilas was young, only eighteen years old, that he had not seen anything of life, he didn't listen and there was nothing they could do. And on July 15, 1945, their wedding was held in the camp. They got a separate room and began to live. They had nothing, so my parents gave them whatever they could spare. In the camp, they also distributed old clothing that they received from America, so little by little we began to dress ourselves. If it didn't fit, we tailored it and we were happy to have it.

Mama was constantly worried that Pranas had not returned. She said that perhaps he was being held captive in some prison. There was a newspaper in our camp. Many people were still searching for members of their families. Because Germany was divided into four parts, we lived in the American Zone. I put an ad in the newspaper that I was searching for my brother Pranas. A few weeks later, I received a letter from the British Zone from Pranas. He had been released from a prisoner-of-war camp in Belgium, as a Lithuanian, so he and another friend from the prison had come to Oldenburg, to the Lithuanian refugee camp there. I immediately wrote to Pranas, told him that our parents were still both alive and that we were all living here in the camp. Tėtis immediately left to bring Pranas back. After a year, we were all together again.

Pranas told us many stories about life in a prisoner-of-war camp. He was very surprised to see that Povilas was married. Anelė would come from Hanau, stay a few days, and then go back again. She very much wanted Pranas to court her, but nothing came of it.

The days passed by uneventfully. We went to dances. I began to see Alfonsas. We would go for walks in the fields, the autumn weather beautiful. On the weekends there were movies or dances. Povilas and Birutė became parents when their daughter was born. Stasys and I were her godparents and baptised her Nijolė.

Our camp had a folk dance ensemble and a chorus, so there were more concerts and plays were staged and there was much laughter and happiness.

Winter passed and in the spring they began to look to see who among the camp's residents should not be allowed to live there. The Russians began pressing all of us to return to Lithuania. And the Lithuanians angrily chased them out of the camp. The Russians then began to say that there were Germans illegally hiding in the camps. The Americans began to check all of the camp's residents, screenings began, everyone had to complete all sorts of forms. Tėtis and Mama had Lithuanian passports, Tėtis had been a volunteer in the Lithuanian army and had fought in the war against Poland over Vilnius. Everything was all right for him, but they kicked about sixty people from the camp then. In a month, we had to go through that same process again. We were all right, nothing changed. One family had to be kicked out of the camp. They went to the office and raised such a fuss, saying that if they were to be kicked out, then they'd say that all of us had been in the German army and they would tell the Americans that we were Nazis. (My brothers Pranas and Povilas had been in the German army, but they were forced to go by the German authorities and were never Nazis.) Well, what could we do. Those masters told us we had to leave the camp in place of that family, because the camp director didn't have much backbone.

Before that, before the screenings, there was a dance ensemble in the camp. Not far from the camp was an American army base, and every Saturday those masters told the female members of the ensemble to go to the American base, to parties, and while those masters sat and partied, those young women were forced to dance with the soldiers. I never went. One day I was called into the director's office. At the time it was a man named Jonas Juodis. When I walked in, he was sitting behind his desk and his secretary was sitting nearby. He asked me why I didn't go to the dances with the Americans. I said I didn't have a pretty dress. The secretary said that she would give me one of hers. I didn't want to say anything more but replied that my father wouldn't allow me to go. The director then said that he would have a talk with my father. We went to see Tėtis. When the director came into the room, he asked my father why he wouldn't let me go. Tėtis answered that his daughter would not go to dance with the soldiers. He added that I was seriously dating Alfonsas and he thought we would get married. The director became quite angry and said to Tėtis that if my father ever needed the director's help, my father should not expect to get it from him. So that's how it came to pass that we had to leave the camp because of that other family and because I would not dance with the Americans.

Once again we had to pack up our belongings. Alfonsas, at the time, was in Kitzingen, working. A truck arrived and loaded us up along with two other families. Birutė remained in the camp with Povilas. It was sad to leave, to give up folk dancing, the ensemble, and so on. Pranas had met a German woman who was living not far from the camp. So he went to live with her and didn't go with us.

They brought us to a small town, to an empty barracks, and we stayed there. After a few days, Alfonsas came to see me. I rejoiced seeing him. He stayed with us until they took us to Untereisenheim, a town not far from the camp, about seven kilometers. And then he often came to visit us.

Birutė was expecting her second daughter. Alfonsas and I wanted to get married, but because neither he nor I were of age, we could not do so without our parents' written permission. My parents didn't want to lose me, to have me go live in the camp while they would have to remain in the village. Alfonsas' parents didn't want him to go live with the Germans while they would emigrate. That's how it went for a time. The two of us decided that we would begin to live together without our parents' permission. We went to the church, we made our promises to one another, and asked God to bless us. We were both very happy. We began to live as if we were married, although Alfonsas still lived in the camp with his parents and I lived with mine. But we were happy that we would not live without one another. We did not say anything to our parents and waited for what would come next.

We learned that we would have to go through a commission in order to return to the camp and that there were also other people who wanted to go back to the camp. We went to Wurzburg. There was a committee there and we had to fill out many forms.

Several months passed and I didn't know what was wrong with me. I started not to feel well. I thought there was something wrong with the food I was eating. That feeling passed. I didn't know that I was expecting a little one. By the time I understood that, the two of us didn't know what to do. I did not say anything to my parents, though when I began to show I told my mother. My parents were angry that I had waited so long to tell them. Alfonsas' parents still didn't want to sign the papers so we could get the registry documents for marriage. And I, by then, didn't want any more worries and I told him that what will be, will be, that we would see. Alfonsas was concerned that I would be all right. And so eventually, on June 26th, a beautiful girl was born. We were so happy that, at last, my labor had ended. Though the girl wasn't yet washed, Alfonsas was kissing her. After she was born, Alfonsas told his parents, and they and his brother Vitas with his wife Aldona came to visit me. They were happy that it was a beautiful girl, and it turns out that Vitas told his parents that this matter needed to be resolved. A week later, they signed the papers that they agreed to our marriage.

I had to stay in bed for five days after giving birth. Mama did everything and I nursed my daughter. I was so happy that

I had a little girl. After a week, I was able to take care of things myself. For my daughter, I had clothes, a carriage. She was a good girl and ate well. Though I didn't have much space, I did have a small room for myself and my daughter. My doctor was a Latvian who lived nearby, so he'd come to visit me. He was a good man.

We began to think about a wedding. Though there were not many responsibilities, we still had to take care of all the documents. We decided on August 10th, in the village church. My parents got more food from the store, a cake, and it was our entire celebration.

That day, Alfonsas' parents, his brother Vitas with Aldona, Alfonsas' sister Onutė with her husband, and Alfonsas' cousin Antanas Vaitkus came to the wedding. When we had to go to the first registry, the witnesses were my doctor and Antanas Vaitkus. After that, we had to go back and get dressed for church. Our attendants were Vitas and Aldona, my brother Pranas with Birutė, Antanas with Pranas' girlfriend Emma, Alfonsas' sister and her husband, and our parents. Everything went well, there were people standing in the street. The priest said a mass, in German. Finally, I became Zdancevičienė. For some reason I didn't feel as if I was no longer an unmarried woman. It seemed to me that that was what was necessary. But when Alfonsas' mother said that there was no longer a Dresliutė (she, in fact, said that I should „stick my maiden name up my ass"), I really wanted to cry.

After lunch, we drove in the doctor's car – I with Alfonsas, Pranas, Birutė, and Emma – but got a flat tire so we had to walk home on foot for a few kilometers. As soon as we returned from church, Vitas and Aldona carried our daughter to church and we baptized her with the names Ramutė Viktorija. Everything all in one day. All went well. It was getting dark and everyone was preparing to go home to Seligenstadt, which was about seven kilometers away. That is how our life together began.

Alfonsas was still working at the camp and received a salary and an increased ration of food, so what I and the little one received was enough for us to eat. Though I had to nurse Ramutė and because the food wasn't necessarily the most nutritious, I lost a lot of weight. After a time, the camp director Jonas Juodis came with his attendants to visit us. He took Ramutė in his arms and said what a beautiful girl she was. He said that we all had to do whatever we could so we could return to the camp. We did not fit in with the Germans and they didn't like foreigners. At that time, a camp had been established in Wurzburg and people began to go through the commissions so they could be allowed to return to the camp. Sometime earlier, the Selingenstadt director was Aušrotas and he liked my family. He was now in charge of that office, so he was able to help many people. We went to see him, he told me what to say, filled out the forms, and only with his assistance were people able to get back into the camp.

And so, after a year and a half, I returned to the camp. My parents also returned with me. They gave us a room where mostly men lived. After a few nights, I could not be there any longer because they partied all night and I could get no rest. Alfonsas went to the office to try to get a different room for us. And a day later we got a new small room for ourselves. It was very narrow and long, so we had to shorten the bed so it could fit at the end of the room. But we had our own room and there was sufficent space because we did not have very much. We had one box for clothes, a box for dishes, and Ramutė's carriage. That was our entire treasure. But we were happy that I was back in the camp and we were no longer at the mercy of the Germans.

Ramutė was already nine months old and ate everything, so there were no problems. They gave milk in the camp – milk specially enriched for children. Alfonsas worked and earned a salary, so we were able to buy some additional things for ourselves. Eventually, we got a different room, a little bit bigger. Alfonsas made a table and we were able to hang our clothes on the wall. But it was an end room, in the barracks, and there was no insulation. I used to stuff the holes in the walls with paper. When winter came, they didn't give us much fuel for the small stove, so while the stove was burning it was warm enough but when it wasn't burning, it got cold quickly. But by then we had a crib for Ramutė, I had featherbedding for her, so she slept warmly. The two of us had an old thick cotton blanket, and at night we put a couple of coats on top and we were able to sleep. As soon as we woke up in the morning, we lit the stove. Alfonsas was working then with the camp police, so at night he would take some wood and that was how we lived.

Tėtis built a little shed and, from the Germans, he bought two small pigs, and we raised them. I didn't do much with them, but my parents fed and looked after them. Pranas did not return to the camp but remained with his Emma. Povilas, when we were still living in the village, had gone to work in the coal mines in Belgium and, it turns out, while there, contracted tuberculosis. When he returned to the camp, he began to cough and it continued to get worse.

When the doctors examined him, they found tuberculosis of the lungs. He was immediately taken to the hospital. Afterwards, they examined his entire family and discovered that his daughter, Nijolė, had tuberculosis of the brain. They took her to the hospital, too, and the girl was very weak. They also took his daughter Danutė and son Algis. They were all in the hospital. Meanwhile, Birutė happily passed the time, found herself some new male friends. Mama went to visit her son and grandchildren in the hospital. It was very sad to see those little children in that situation, alone in the hospital. The doctor said that Mama needed to tell Birutė to come to the hospital and to look after her children. She eventually went and spent time with them. Povilas ended up in the Nuremberg Sanatorium. The children were also taken to that place, so Birutė ended up there with all of her stuff as well.

Before that, when we got that larger room, Alfonsas had been working with the camp police. He later got a job in Schweinfurt, in a transit camp, because emigration had started since the Germans no longer wanted to look after foreigners. I spent the summer alone with Ramutė. It was 1948. Alfonsas would come home, bring his earnings, would stay for a day, and then would leave again. It wasn't far, about twenty kilometers. My parents lived right here so they helped me a lot. My brother Pranas lived in a village not far from the camp. When he came to visit one day he told my parents that he would be getting married on August 8. My parents did not want him to remain there. They wanted him to come with them to America or maybe Australia. He told them that he was remaining in Germany and did not want to go anywhere else. My parents pleaded and wept, but he did not listen to them. His wedding was in Volkach. The only ones there were us, my parents, and Povilas and his wife. Emma's mother made lunch, and when we returned from the church we ate, sat for a bit, and the party was over. Emma's mother wasn't one of the good ones and Pranas knew it would be difficult. Though Pranas and Emma lived in the village and had more food than we did, they never helped my parents, and we didn't have very much food of our own.

Summer passed. Our barracks had been built for German soldiers but they became infested with bed bugs. People tried to clean the barracks on their own but they didn't have the proper equipment. One day, Germans arrived with machines, told everyone to take their clothes outside, sealed the windows and doors, and sprayed the barracks with sulphur. Those who had somewhere to sleep that night went there, but others had to sleep on their clothes on the ground outside all night. Ramutė and I spent the time with my parents. After a day, we were allowed to return. It was much better, though it still smelled of sulphur. But the bed bugs were all eliminated.

People began to emigrate. Everyone wanted to go to America. But it was not that easy to get there. It was necessary to have someone who would claim you, guarantee a job and housing, pay travel expenses. Because we didn't have relatives in America, we didn't think we would get there. The one way out for us was to emigrate to Australia. We filled out the forms and were waiting until we were called to the commission. Alfonsas' father bumped into an acquaintance of his who asked him where we were planning to go. My father-in-law said Australia. His friend asked why not to America and said that there was a way. He told my father-in-law where to get the forms. He got them for all of us. They were forms that indicated that if we agreed to work for a farmer for a year, then we could emigrate to America. We completed everything we needed to fill out and waited for them to call us. My father-in-law's chance meeting with someone he knew on the sidewalk changed our lives.

They began to close the camp then and we had to travel to Wurzburg. They established a camp there for those who were preparing to emigrate, no matter to where. I was assigned a small room with Ramutė. They gave us food in the cafeteria. Alfonsas was still with the Schweinfurt police. My parents and Alfonsas' parents were here with us. The days passed monotonously. Alfonsas would come and stay for a couple of days and then leave again. Because I had time, Ramutė and I would go to the Main River and sit together. I had time, so I read a lot. To go to America, you had to be able to read and write. Tėtis began to read so, if necessary, he could demonstrate that he could read. When he was young he didn't go to school very much because there was a war on [World War I] and he voluteered for the army when he was seventeen. When he was much younger, he had to help his mother to support their family. He was still a child and had

43

to work because his father had died and his mother was left with eleven children, all still young. So that's how he ended up not going to school. Now he tried to read, and I helped him. Mama was not without education and had loved to read since she was a girl. She was also a seamstress, so she had to write and add numbers, too.

Povilas was in the hospital, his children were in the hospital, all in Nuremberg. Pranas remained with his wife. In the village, only Stasys and I were with our parents. Finally, our turn to begin the journey came. In Schweinfurt was the transit camp, the consulate, doctors. Once again I packed my boxes with what I had. Because we were going with Alfonsas' parents as a single family, we had to go everywhere together. Though I didn't want to do that, what else could I do? Alfonsas arrived and loaded our things on to the truck. It wasn't far, about an hour to Schweinfurt. They dropped us off and we ended up in one room with his parents. Alfonsas was still working so he ate in the kitchen. Ramutė got food from the children's kitchen, so it wasn't bad for me either. There were many people, all of them wanting to leave as soon as possible. Vitas and Aldona lived nearby, so I would visit them as well.

We had to go through all sorts of offices, doctors, the consul. They checked our healths. If you had something wrong with your lungs, you could not go to America. We successfully passed everything, they found no illnesses among us. We waited for them to call us to the consulate. Our turn came and it wasn't as bad as some people thought. There was a fairly young American and he didn't ask us too many things. He wished us a good trip and our journey's hardships came to an end.

Alfonsas was still working and got clothing for the trip from the police, so we sold everything and had some money for our journey. We went to see my parents. They had not yet been called to the transit camp. It was hard to say good-bye because the road was long and we didn't know when we would see each other again. When we learned that we would be taken to Wildflecken, we all got together at Vitas and Aldona's. They were staying behind because their son had just been born. We sat with them for a while and then we had to go pack our belongings for our journey to America.

One morning, trucks arrived and loaded our things. We said good-bye to Vitas and Aldona, to our friends, and began our journey to America. A few hours later, we were in Wildflecken. They gave us a room together with others, we ate again in a cafeteria, and though there was not a lot of food, there was enough to keep us from starvation. Because we had some money, we added some bread or perhaps a fish. We were not there for long. I liked it there because it was a beautiful town and we took many walks through it. We were there for just two weeks and we had to leave for Gronau, not far from the sea.

Once again we traveled by truck. They brought us to Gronau, to a large camp filled with people of many nationalities. They gave us a room with many other women. Men were separated from their families. Ramutė and I were given one bed to share, but I was fine with that. We didn't have many things with us because they had taken our larger boxes to a warehouse. And again we ate in a cafeteria. The food was always the same. In the morning they gave us two slices of bread with margarine. For lunch, soup or potatoes with gravy, with very small pieces of meat. In the evening, we got bread again with a slice of sausage. We were always hungry. Ramutė received separate rations. While we still had money, I would buy Ramutė a roll or an apple. We would walk near the river and, sitting there, would think that we didn't need much, that all we wanted was a small house and five hundred dollars in the bank when we were in America.

It was harder for me when I had to wash our clothes. The laundry was in a cellar and there were many women there. I had to take Ramutė with me but she didn't want to stay there. We did not go to where Alfonsas was living with the men and he came to see us only when it was time for lunch. My mother-in-law wandered through the fields and never asked me if I needed any help. I got angry once and told Alfonsas that he had to come in the morning and take the girl. There were many such occurences, but it's not possible to write them all down here. It was hard because, though we didn't have much clothing with us, I still had to have clean underwear for Ramutė and for us, so I washed and made sure they were clean. I tried to do all I could without any help. Though I was in the same room with my mother-in-law, she looked after only herself. And I knew not to expect any help from her. I made do without her.

In that camp were people from many countries and all went to eat in the same cafeteria, but the Jews had their own dining hall and, when I passed by, it smelled so good. It seems they got better food, ate as much as they wanted, but we were given just enough to keep from starving.

After lunch we'd walk down the street near the camp and there were many shops there, filled with everything we could have wanted, but we saved as much as we could so there would be enough each day to buy a roll or some fruit for Ramutė. But we were young and knew that this was just a temporary situation. Ramutė was already two years old, fairly heavy, but she went to no one else, only to me, and I had to carry her. Whenever we went for a walk, she would get tired and would tell me to carry her. I was just barely a little over a hundred pounds, but what could I do when my daughter was crying? I carried her. She wouldn't even go to her father.

Two weeks passed and they started to put our documents in order because more and more people were arriving in the transit camp every day. Finally, they told us to gather in the yard with our things. They checked our papers and we climbed into a bus which took us to the train station.

The train was already there, we climbed aboard, they loaded our boxes, and we went back to the journey.

They took us to the port city of Bremerhaven. They checked our papers again and we climbed off the train. There was a big ship there, the General Howze. After our documents were checked, they finally let us onto the ship. I got a small cabin with Ramutė. Alfonsas was put into a large room below deck with all the other men. They separated families. In my room were two bunk beds, a closet, and a bathroom. We were able to open the window because it was on the first deck. My roommates were a Jewish woman with a child and her mother. My bed was the lower bunk, so that's where Ramutė and I slept. I was content.

I arranged my things. The room was small but there was enough space for us. My roommate was a nice woman and her child was Ramutė's age. She understood only a little Lithuanian, so we spoke in Polish. It was especially good to have our own bathroom. Though it was small, we could bathe under a shower. So I immediately bathed Ramutė and washed myself as well.

A little while later, they told us to go to the dining hall to eat, only women and children. It was a very beautiful place, men waited on us, the food was good and we could eat as much as we wanted, and the coffee was delicious. Ramutė could have as much milk as she wanted.

After we ate, we went on the deck to watch how they were loading the ship. Alfonsas met us there. He was living below in the ship, with only men, and there were too few bathrooms for so many. So when he needed, he came to use ours. We stood on the deck and the ship began to move, slowly sailing away from the harbor. I don't know how to write down the emotion I felt watching the shore recede. Tears filled my eyes. I knew we were sailing to America, and here remained my parents, my brothers, and I didn't know if they would pass by the commission and come to us. It was very hard to leave all that behind. Even though it had been hard in all the camps, at least we had been together. And though now Alfonsas' parents were here in the ship, we were not sailing to the same place. Only my daughter and I were sailing together, and what we would find there we did not know.

Front cover, Janina at the age of 17.

1. Janina's parents, Viktorija Župerkaitė and Arturas Dreslius, on their wedding day, May 25, 1924.
2. Janina at the age of four, with her parents and brothers Pranas (l.) and Povilas (r.)
3. Janina's younger sister Marytė, who died at the age of six months.
4. Janina in the middle of the front row, with her parents (on the left), her aunt and uncle (on the right), and her favorite cousin Marytė in the middle behind her.
5. Janina's First Communion class, Spring 1935.
6. One of the houses in which Janina lived in 1936 with her family, in Petrašiūnai.
7. Janina's father, Arturas, third from the left in the long apron, working in the paper mill, 1936.
8. Janina holding a long wreath at a military celebration, late 1930s. She is in the first row, the third child from the right.
9. Janina at school in the summer of 1939. She is in the second row, second from the left, in a dark dress, embracing her teacher.
10. Janina with her sister-in-law Birutė and friends, in the Displaced Persons camp, mid-1940s.
11. Janina and Alfonsas on their wedding day, August 10, 1947.
12. Alfonsas serving in the camp police.
13. Alfonsas and Janina in the camp.
14. Janina's family in the camp: (l. to r.) sister-in-law Birutė holding her daughter; brother Pranas and his wife Emma; Janina's mother holding Ramutė, with Alfonsas in back of them; Janina; Janina's brother Stasys; Janina's father; and in the back, Janina's brother Povilas holding his daughter.
15. On the farm in Vermont.
16. The family, Spring 1959.
17. The Maple Motel.
18. Janina and Alfonsas in Dotnuva (during their first return trip to Lithuania in 1989), at her grandfather's house, where she spent her summers as a young girl.
19. Janina in front of the house in Petrašiūnai where she lived in the mid-1930s.
20. Janina referred to her children in this photograph as "Our Quartet."
21. Their last photograph together, taken on October 22, 2016, two months before Alfonsas died.

Back cover, Walking together again.

PART TWO

Coming to America

We were going to a farmer, to work on a farm. The ship sailed calmly, it didn't rock, and I was happy it was a good journey. Before reaching the shores of England, we had dinner. The food was delicious, we ate a lot, and I even took some for Ramutė to have later because it was only about six o'clock in the evening. We stood on the deck for a little while and it was time for Ramutė to go to sleep. I laid down next to her. The ship rocked a little but nothing much and we slept soundly.

We went to eat breakfast the next morning. Alfonsas had been taken to work in the kitchen and he was quite happy because he ate well and the food was good. His job wasn't hard. Lunch was also good. The cafeteria was a fine place. They waited on us politely and all the waiters liked Ramutė and would bring her something delicious. One of the cooks, a Filipino, came to us and brought Ramutė some orange chocolate. He would distribute it to the children and they all would wait happily for him.

I would walk on the deck with Ramutė and it was completely terrifying to look at that ocean. In the evening, Alfonsas came and we stayed for a little while on the deck and it was again time for bed. That night I felt that the boat was rocking a bit more.

In the morning we went to have breakfast but I wasn't able to eat much at all. We spent most of our time in the cabin and my roommate began to get sick. I went to lunch with my daughter because the little girl wanted to eat. She ate but I didn't want any food. I brought a little back to the cabin for her. In the evening, the boat was rocking even more and Ramutė liked it. I barely made it to the dining hall but hurried back. I didn't eat anything. Ramutė ate well. At night the ship really began to rock and I didn't sleep at all. In the morning, my daughter wanted to eat. I started to go to the dining hall with her, but when I saw that the corridor was dropping down and then lifting up, I immediately returned to the cabin and climbed into bed. Alfonsas came and got Ramutė and took her to the dining room. They didn't want to let men in but saw that I wasn't there and allowed him. Ramutė ate and Alfonsas returned to work. At lunch he brought fresh tomatoes and sauerkraut and I lived on those for three days.

    I couldn't go anywhere and mostly stayed in bed with Ramutė. My father-in-law said that my mother-in-law was very sick. He wasn't sick and spent most of his time walking on the deck. Her sons just up and brought their mother to my cabin. She looked as if she wouldn't survive. They put her into my bed and Ramutė and I climbed up onto the top bunk. An American woman came to check the rooms and saw that my mother-in-law was here, so she told her that she had to return to the women's room, that this wasn't the place for her. She brought in a man and another one, a soldier, and he asked me if I agreed for her to be in the room. I said I wasn't opposed, so they left her with me. A couple of days later, the weather calmed down and I was able to go out onto the deck. Though I wasn't able to eat, I could drink tea. Alfonsas would bring something from the kitchen and that's how I survived.

    In the evenings, after I put Ramutė to bed, I would go out on to the deck. How terrifying it was to look into the black water. We sailed for nine days. Eventually, they came to check our documents again, and the ship stopped just outside New York. We saw the Statue of Liberty from a distance. It was such a strange feeling that we were now here, in this place, in America.

    We woke at four o'clock in the morning. We had to go through all the document checks again and they examined our papers and finally, at around noon, the ship sailed into the harbor. Once again, we lined up and they checked our last names and began to let passengers off the ship. How wonderful it was to walk on ground that didn't rock under our feet. It was August 10, 1949.

We were met by a woman representative from the refugee organization. She told us that they would be putting us on a train and that we would be going to Vermont. It took some time before they unloaded all of the baggage from the ship. It was the first time that we saw women from the „Blue Cross." They gave us each a bagel and some coffee. It was very warm outside and we weren't accustomed to the humidity and Ramutė got very sweaty. A couple of Lithuanian women from that organization took Ramutė and washed and changed her.

We waited again until we passed all of the control points. We wanted to rest because we hadn't slept all night, but we were finally taken by one of those representatives – her name was Valaitytė – and she and a man took us out to dinner in a restaurant after we said good-bye to Alfonsas' parents. We were going to Westford, Vermont, near Burlington, and they were being taken to Putney. After we ate, they drove us to the train station. I found it very strange that there was so much trash in the streets, papers blown everywhere by the wind. They took us to the station, we put our baggage alongside our suitcases on a bench, and Ramutė immediately fell asleep.

They bought tickets for us to White River Junction. They gave Alfonsas fifteen dollars for our trip – five dollars for each of us, our first money in America – and left us at the station to wait until it was time for the train. They told us to which platform we would have to go at seven o'clock that evening. So we stayed in the station, not understanding the language.

Because there was still time before the train left, I went to buy some grapes because we were quite thirsty. For the first time in my life then I saw a black woman and her children. Ramutė woke up and Alfonsas went for a walk with her. I sat with our suitcases barely able to keep my eyes open, I was so exhausted. Finally, seven o'clock came and a station official came up to us and said it was time to board the train. As soon as we put up our baggage and the train began to move, I fell alseep. We had to travel all night, so all of us fell asleep.

We slept well, but I woke up early in the morning and, as the train started to move again, I saw that we were leaving the station we were supposed to get out in. Well, what could we do. We went on to the next one. The man who had been waiting for us at the station saw that we didn't climb out and drove on to the next station as well. When we arrived at that station, we climbed out onto the platform. We waited to see what would happen next. At the station they noticed that we didn't speak English. We sat and waited until someone would pick us up. The people at the station brought us coffee and cookies. They said for us to go to the store because the people there spoke a different language. Alfonsas went and said „good morning" in Lithuanian and those people just looked at him. They were French.

He came back and the man arrived to pick us up. He had a beautiful car. He had seen that we had not gotten out at White River Junction so he followed the train here. We got into his car and our trip to Westford began. We drove down very beautiful roads. Vermont is beautiful. He picked a newspaper off his seat and showed us the article that had been written about us. We were the first D.P. [Displaced Persons] Lithuanians to come to work on Vermont's farms. We stopped at a store and he bought Ramutė some ice cream, she said it was delicious. It's very uncomfortable when you don't know the language and can't communicate. I asked him, the best I could, what other languages he spoke and he said only French. So we sat there quietly until we arrived at our designated place.

The family we were delivered to were LaCasse – their last name – and both were still quite young. They met us in the yard. We went into their kitchen. It was a big kitchen but very messy, all sorts of clothes thrown everywhere, the table top dirty, the cabinets stuffed with newspapers and other things.

The entry hall was filled with all sorts of things, bones too, and was also very messy. Well, finally, we were at our place.

We didn't have much with us because our baggage only arrived a few days later. They took us to the second floor. There were three rooms. In one was a bed and a crib, in the kitchen was a stove and a small table, and the third was empty. This was our apartment.

After lunch, Alfonsas and the landlord went to a neighboring farm to cut down a tree. I remained with Ramutė. We went outside and I spread a blanket on the grass and Ramutė fell asleep. I was very tired but sat there and looked around the farm. A couple of hours later, Ramutė woke up. The climate was very different here, hot and humid. I didn't have a change of clothes so I wore the same outfit for two days and nights. Some people arrived when I was sitting there. The man was a professor from Washington and they were on vacation here. He started to talk with me but I didn't understand him. Then he started to speak in German. I was so happy that we would be able to talk. They were very nice people. They took Ramutė and me to the store to buy food. They bought a lot for us and it took a couple of hours until we returned. It was wonderful to talk with them. They asked many things about Lithuania, about Germany. His people were from there. They promised to come back to visit again, and though their vacation was ending, we did see them a few more times.

Alfonsas came back in the evening with the landlord. His name was Raymond and his wife was a Spanish woman, very beautiful. We had not slept for two nights, we were all exhausted, so we immediately went to sleep. Very early the next morning, at five o'clock, there was a knock on the door, it was time to go milk the cows. Ramutė and I stayed in bed until the cows were milked and then went downstairs to the landlords' to have breakfast. They gave us each a small bowl of Cheerios and a slice of bread with cheese and some coffee. We weren't used to that sort of food.

Alfonsas and Raymond then went to the forest to cut wood. I went with my daughter to clean up our room but the landlady wanted me to clean her rooms, so I became a maid. When I saw how much needed to be done before I finished it all, and because I didn't have clothes suitable to do that work, I couldn't do much that day. Two days later, our baggage arrived. It was then better and easier because I was able to dress myself and Ramutė properly for the heat and humidity. It was August 12 and we weren't accustomed to either. In the evenings, when we went to bed, we would open the windows and listen to the noises the frogs or grasshoppers made. There were no neighbors nearby. I was afraid to sleep. No one locked the doors here, everything was open.

In the morning. once again, it was time to milk the cows. After breakfast, Ramutė would play with their daughter. She was three years old and was named Sheila. I started to clean the kitchen. There was a great deal of work, nothing had been cleaned for a long time. I washed the walls, the windows, the cabinets. It took a few days until I was able to get to washing the floors. When he came back from working, her husband couldn't believe that the floor had such a nice color. I was not very strong and it was very hot, so I would get tired quickly.

We didn't get paid for six weeks because the landlords had paid for our trip from the boat to Westford, so we had to pay them back because we should have paid for our trip ourselves but we didn't have any money. Mr. Jenkinson arrived from Burlington. He was a Lithuanian who had been born here and belonged to the Union, in fact he was the steward. It was nice to talk to him. He concerned himself with the condition of immigrants. He found out that Alfonsas' sister Onutė had arrived at a farm not far from us, about fifteen kilometers away. So he called the farmer and told him to bring them to visit us. They came that Sunday. It was wonderful to see them again after so much time. They weren't very happy, but they did live separately from the farm where they worked. They had gotten their own house. Onutė didn't have to work because her two daughters were still young and they couldn't be left on their own.

Jenkinson called one day and said that my parents had already arrived, at a farm quite far from us, in the town of Rupert, near Rutland, Vermont. Alfonsas' parents also ended up quite far from us. I wrote to my parents. I very much wanted to see them. Onutė also wanted to see her parents. The two of us decided to go. Her farmer brought her and her girls to me and my farmer drove us to the bus station in Burlington. The farmer had a thirty-two year old small truck, so we and the girls sat in the back of the truck and he and his wife sat in the truck's cab. We thought it was quite funny. We had gotten all dressed up and here we were sitting in the bed of the truck on top of a bunch of bags. But we were happy they were bringing us.

We arrived at the bus station and bought tickets. Though I didn't know the language well yet and pronouced words not as they should be, we were brave and traveled happily. The trip was a long one. The driver knew we didn't know the language but I showed him the address. He brought us to Putney and we wanted to get out but he said no. We drove on a little bit further and he stopped in the middle of the fields, pointed to a farm, and said to go there. We climbed out and began to walk toward the farm and we saw Jonas and Algis running to meet us. When we got there, Alfonsas' parents greeted us. There was lots of talk and we told each other about everything that had happened during the time we hadn't seen each other. I stayed a couple of days and then traveled on to see my parents.

I arrived in Rutland, climbed out of the bus with Ramutė, but didn't know where to go next. I saw a sign „Drugstore" across the street, went there, and picked up a telephone book to try to find the last name Lewis, which was the name of my parents' farmer. But there were so many of them. Ramutė began to cry, tired of sitting there. The salesgirl saw us and asked me where I was going. I showed her the address. She told me to give it to her and she would call. She soon returned and said to wait, that someone would be coming to pick us up. She brought me some coffee and cake and brought Ramutė some milk and cookies. We waited for about an hour. A lady came in and told me to go outside to the car. I went out and saw that Mama was sitting in the car, and I was so happy that I was at last where I was supposed to be.

We drove for quite a while. The farmer lived in the village of Rupert and it was already dark when we arrived. Tėtis and Stasys were milking the cows, and when they came up we hugged each other and we were so happy to see one another again. They drove us to the house where my parents lived, not far from the woods, about a mile down the road. The house was old and broken down, and I don't know how my parents could have lived there. Well, now Ramutė and I would stay here, too.

In the morning, when I woke up, it wasn't as terrible as it first seemed. The woods were beautiful, there were many apple trees. Though everything was very old, tattered, Mama fixed up what she could and it was possible to live there. Early in the morning, Tėtis and Stasys went to the farm to milk the cows. Ramutė and I went for a walk in the woods. We then went to the farm. The landlady was very nice, gave us some cookies. Mama said she was afraid to live in that house, that it was possible cowboys would come and shoot them. When we were still living in Germany, after the Americans came and we were already in the camp, they would show films every week, mostly about cowboys. And they were always shooting each other. Mama thought the woods were full of cowboys.

I had been staying with my parents for about a week when, on Saturday, I saw a car pull up and Alfonsas climbed out, together with Jenkinson and his girlfriend. Jenkinson asked how my parents liked living here, and he said he did not like the house when he saw it. He asked how the farmer was treating them, too. Tėtis was not happy with that old farmer, who did not like foreigners at all. Though he and Stasys were both good workers, that old farmer never liked what they did and did not pay them their wages. Jenkinson talked to the old farmer but nothing improved. The farmer's son was a good man and he did everything he could so it could be better for my parents. Alfonsas said it was time for us to go back, though Mama pleaded that I at least leave Ramutė with her. She said she would then not be so sad and lonely. I had to go back with Alfonsas, because our farmer did not let him out for long. I left Ramutė behind, though it was hard to do so, but only so Mama would not be alone.

We drove for a long time. Jenkinson bought dinner for us in a restaurant. We talked a lot about the lives of Lithuanians in Vermont. He kept telling us that he would help us buy a farm and we would remain there forever. Although we weren't especially interested in that, we agreed with him and pretended that we would be content with what he suggested.

We returned home quite late and then went back to the same routine. Milking the cows, cutting trees in the woods. I had to help my landlady because she was expecting a baby. I got tired of all those farm jobs. My parents called and said that their farmer wasn't paying them and they had no money to buy food. We immediately called Jenkinson. That old farmer was very bad. Tėtis and Stasys stopped going to work because he wasn't paying them. We sent them ten dollars so they could buy food for Ramutė. Jenkinson went to see them and talked to the farmer. The son said that his father would no longer interfere in the work Tėtis and Stasys were doing and that they should come back to work. But when they returned to work, the old man was the same.

Tėtis's sister, Greta, lived in New York state, near Plattsburgh. So when Mama wrote her a letter and explained everything that was going on, she came immediately and took my parents to live with her. That old farmer begged them to stay, but my parents would not agree. A few days later, I saw a car pulling into the yard and Mama, Ramutė, and Aunt Greta climbed out. I was so happy that Ramutė was home again, because I was worried about where she would end up. They stay for a few hours and, after eating, left.

My parents were living temporarily at Greta's farmer's, but there wasn't much work there so they found employment with another farner, named Penke, outside of Plattsburgh. He was of German ancestry, had a large farm and many animals. Tėtis and Stasys together earned fifty dollars a week. They had their own apartment near Lake Champlain. It was a very beautiful place.

Because Ramutė was home again, the two of us would go to the woods to gather mushrooms. There were many of them, including summer boletes [baravykai]. I tried to dry them but they rotted. I didn't know how to prepare them for drying.

My landlady had a washing machine and washed everything together in the same water. So her clothes were more black than white. I found a washboard in the barn and I washed my own clothing. But because there was no water to rinse them with, I would carry my laundry in buckets to a stream not far from the farm – it was small and its water was clean – and would wash it there. I would hang the washed clothes to dry on a wire we had stretched out in the yard.

When Alfonsas received his first wages, we went to the store to buy groceries for ourselves. It was so good to prepare our own food. We ate and rejoiced that we had our own ham, bacon, eggs. Because our landlady didn't know how to cook, we had mostly been eating hot dogs and peas. They butchered a pig and I took the head and feet, because they were throwing them out. For the first time in my life, I cooked aspic [košeliena], using the entire head and feet. It came out pretty tasty but it was so hard and thick that it could only be cut with a big knife. We did not have a refrigerator, so after a couple of days I had to throw it out.

Not far from our farm lived a single woman. She was old already and I would go visit her. We talked a lot and she helped me a great deal with my English language. Every Sunday, we would go to church one at a time, because we had to work even on Sundays. The priest would also cone to see us. He brought us a radio and some pictures for the walls, and it was quite good to talk with him. Occasionally, Onutė would come over with her family. Alfonsas and I would ride our bicycles to visit them, too. It wasn't far, about twenty miles. Neighboring farmers would also come by and bring us to their homes for lunch. They would say that the farm looked much better now that we were there. That was because Alfonsas cleaned everything. The barn had been in such a condition that you couldn't walk through it past all of the spiderwebs. Around the house you couldn't walk without almost breaking your legs. Everything now was clean and we were able even to sit in the yard.

A reporter from *Life Magazine* arrived one day and took many photographs, asking us if we were content and happy. But he could see that we were not farmers. Alfonsas worked hard. He would get up at five every morning, milked the cows, cleaned the barn, after breakfast went to the woods to cut trees, went back to the barn after he came back from the woods, and so on until evening. We knew that this would be for only one year, because according to our entry agreement and visa, we had to work only for one year on that farm.

The landlady was close to giving birth, so mostly I did everything. There were gardens and I took whatever could be eaten. The summer corn was delicious, though we didn't eat much of it. I cooked what we preferred to eat. Though I had to cook separately for them, and I had to take care of two kitchens. At last, they took her to the hospital and she gave birth to a boy, but he was not healthy, so they left him in the hospital. She come home a week later but did nothing, though she was able to, because she knew that I would do it all. And then later, a little bit at a time, she began to straighten up her rooms. They took her child to a hospital in Boston, so they traveled there and Alfonsas and I took care of the farm. They picked up the milk in the mornings and took it to a big dairy. We always had fresh milk, though it was not pasteurized.

Some time later the farmer said that they would butcher a cow, so there would be enough meat for the winter. Alfonsas knew how to butcher animals, and they took the meat to a town freezer because they didn't have sufficient room in their refrigerator to freeze it all. We ate whatever meat they gave us and considered ourselves lucky that we didn't have to buy it. The farmer didn't have any money so he hadn't paid Alfonsas for three weeks already. That's how a few weeks passed.

There was a big farm not far away and he had many cows. When the time came to herd them back into the barn, he couldn't find one of his cows. He asked Alfonsas if he and our farmer had butchered a large cow. He went to the town freezer and found out how much meat our farmer had stored. Alfonsas told our farmer that they were searching for that cow. Our farmer got very confused and said that he had butchered his own cow. I called Jenkinson and told him what had happened. He told me not to be afraid, that we were only workers and that we did what we were told to do. He said that he would transfer us to a different farm, where Alfonsas would have to drive milk to the central dairy. We were happy that the job would be an easier one.

I called my parents immediately. The next day, the other farmer came to take Ramutė and me to Burlington to go shopping. We left right after breakfast. It was good to walk around the shops and I bought a few things for myself and for

Ramutė. We also went out to eat. The time passed quickly. It was already dark when we returned. I saw that a truck was standing in the yard. My brother Stasys and his farmer. All of our things had already been packed up. Alfonsas said we had to leave immediately because the ferry to go across the lake ran only until six p.m. and my parents lived near Plattsburgh. I did not even have time to go to our rooms. I just told our landlady goodbye and we got into the truck.

Stasys told us that when they learned that our farmer had butchered another farmer's cow, his farmer said that they should go get us and bring us back there. He said they would find jobs for us. That was December 3, 1949. Ramutė and I sat in the cab of the truck while Alfonsas and Stasys sat on top. It was very cold and they had a big blanket, and that's how we traveled.

When we got to the ferry, it was already too late. We had to go around to take the bridge. He stopped at a store and bought some milk and cookies for Ramutė, some wine for the men so they wouldn't freeze. We were very tired because we didn't reach my parents until late that night. Mama had already made supper for us, had made the beds. Though we were exhasted, we ate and then collapsed into our beds. We slept well.

When I woke early in the morning the weather was good, it was sunny, the lake was right here. It was a beautiful place. The farmer was a German and spoke German. Tėtis was very happy here, there were many cows to milk. He and Stasys helped that farmer a lot. They built a barn, cleaned everywhere, and everything was in good order. On the first floor lived a Lithuanian family. They had come to that farm earlier. Alfonsas helped with the farm work, we lived with my parents, so we didn't have very many worries. After a while, he told us that we would have to find a place of our own because he had enough workers already. For Christmas we went with Alfonsas and Stasys to see Alfonsas' parents. Stasys was friends with Alfonsas' brother Algis. I threw up on the bus trip. I didn't know what could be wrong with me. I thought that perhaps I had eaten the wrong food. The time there passed nicely and we returned to Plattsburgh. Just after New Year's, we got a job with another farmer, namd LaBier, not far from my parents. The house wasn't bad. His daughter with her family lived upstairs. We had three rooms. The toilet was outside, in the kitchen there was a water pump to get water. It was cold in there, though they gave us wood. While it burned, it was warm enough but it cooled off quickly once the fire went out. It was so cold that water froze in the kitchen. But we were content.

One day, when we were at my parents', Jenkinson arrived with the Vermont and New York police. I was very afraid what would happen. Was it because we had left that farmer or because of that cow? They were very pleasant and asked about the cow. When it was butchered, where were the head and hooves buried? Alfonsas told them everything. A few days earlier, our former farmer. Raymond, had come and brought us what he owed Alfonsas for his work, about sixty dollars, and told us that the police had been to see him and that he told them he had not butchered any cow. He said that if Alfonsas said anything to the police he would kill him. We were very afraid and Alfonsas told that to the police as well while Jenkinson translated because it was still difficult to speak in English. They told him not to be afraid, that he did not know whose cow that was, and that he did what he was told to do. They stayed with us for a little while, asked how we liked the work, saw that we were still young and had just started our lives. They wished us well and gave us a telephone number to let them know immediately if anyone threatened us. That's how the history of the cow ended.

Jenkinson was not very happy that we had left Vermont, asked why we hurried away, said that he would have found jobs for us. He very much wanted us to be farmers and there were many farms for sale in Vermont then. But we didn't want to work on a farm for the rest of our lives. We later read in the newspaper, in an article Jenkinson had written, that a farmer had been sentenced and would be spending time in jail. He, too, had just begun his life and he had to serve out his sentence. He ruined his name in the farming community.

We began to live at LaBier's. Alfonsas worked from five in the morning until seven at night. He earned twenty dollars a week. We bought our own food in Plattsburgh but the farmer gave us potatoes and milk. I began not to feel well. I couldn't eat. They took me to the doctor, who was an old Lithuanian. He examined me and told me that I was pregnant. I told Alfonsas and we decided that everything would be all right, that we would have a second child. The winter was cold. We needed a lot of fuel because I didn't go anywhere and we piled the wood up on the veranda. Someone would bring me and Ramutė to my parents'. We would stay for a few days. Once I was going to the cellar and fell down the stairs. I was very afraid that I would lose the baby, but I stayed in bed for a few days and everything was all right.

That's how the days passed. At least once a month the farmer's son would drive us to the movies. We received a letter from Alfonsas' parents that it turned out that there were some relatives, on the Zdancevičius side, living in New Britain, Connecticut. They had come to Vermont to visit and promised to take Alfonsas' brother Jonas with them and then later his parents, too. So in March, Jonas was already in New Britain. He got a job and found a place to live, so Alfonsas' parents went to live with their son. Sometime later, Onutė and her family also went to her parents. She didn't want to work on a farm any longer.

We were still living at LaBier's. In April, Alfonsas said that he would go to his parents and that I should go to mine, until he found a job and he would then get us both. He said he would find a place to live and we could then begin our lives in a city where there were more Lithuanians and more events and a Lithuanian church. So he decided that he would leave for New Britain in early May.

We had to tell our farmer that we were going to leave. He got very angry because, in the spring, there were many jobs to do in the fields. But we were prepared to go and my parents' farmer arrived and drove the three of us to my parents. Alfonsas left a few days later to go to his parents and I remained with mine. There wasn't much for me to do, so I spent my time walking with Ramutė by the lake and waited for letters from my husband. He would write to say that he was looking for work but that, at the time, there were not many jobs available. Our time passed quickly. Tėtis worked a great deal with Stasys, the farmer wanted them to work all day on Sundays as well but they were so exhausted that they would not agree.

I had been at my parents' for three weeks when I received a letter from Alfonsas that he had found a job, so I was very happy and wanted to go to him as quickly as possible. My parents' farmer wanted them to pay for me because I was living with them, but I told him that I was going to Alfonsas. So I packed my suitcase, took Ramutė, and a neighbor drove us to the Plattsburgh train station.

I was already almost eight months pregnant, so the trip was a difficult one. We got to Troy, New York, and we had to take a taxi to go to a different station to get on the train to Springfield, Massachusetts. By the time I got a taxi, we didn't get to the other station on time so we had to wait for a few hours until the next train. It was already late. I arrived in Springfield, Massachusetts. I got out of the train and was walking with Ramutė. I didn't know where to go. Then I heard some women and a man speaking in Lithuanian. I asked them how to get to New Britain. They said that there were no more trains there today, but there would be a bus. They saw that I was pregnant and had a small girl, so they said they would help me. One picked up Ramutė and carried her, the other one took my suitcase, and they drove us in their car to the bus station. I bought a ticket, thanked them, and they showed me which bus to take. They said it would take about an hour to get to New Britain. Ramutė fell asleep and I was also very tired, but what could I do, we had to travel.

  We arrived in Hartford and I got off on Main Street. It was already late and it was the last bus going to New Britain. I stood there for a while and then saw a bus coming and „New Britain" was written on it. I climbed in, gave the driver a dollar, and he gave me change. So I sat down. He called me up and told me to drop twenty cents into the automatic coin catcher. And so we were traveling again.

  We arrived in New Britain, on Main Street. That driver saw that I didn't know where to go, and it was already after eleven o'clock at night, so he stopped a taxi and I gave him the address of Alfonsas' parents. He brought us to a house on Spring Street. I gave him a dollar, telling him that I didn't have any more, and he took it and drove off.

  The house was two stories high and everything was dark. I knocked on the door of the first floor, and after a while a woman asked me what I wanted. I told her the last name and she told me to go into the backyard, up to the second floor. I just could no longer carry my suitcase. I picked up Ramutė and the two of us climbed the stairs to the second floor. The door wasn't locked, there was a small lamp buring near the table. I went inside and started calling „mama". Immediately, my mother-in-law and father-in-law came into the room, very surprised that I had come so late. Jonas and Algis also came, but my husband wasn't there. I asked where he was, and they told me that he had gone out to drink beer with his friends. It was a Friday. Jonas went over to the Vyšniauskas' place. In the second building there was a beer hall, and he told my husband that I had arrived. Alfonsas was quite surprised and he came quickly. He said he didn't know that I would be coming. We sat for a while and I finally went to bed.

Alfonsas began to look for an apartment because I very much wanted to have a place of my own. We had to find a place because shortly there would be a newborn. I had been there for a week. We went to see Onutė, who didn't live too far from here. Alfonsas was looking for a place to live every day. With him went Juozas Dlugauskas. Finally, after a long search, we got our own apartment in a house owned by some old Lithuanians named Šiugžda. It had two bedrooms. I didn't go looking for apartments anywhere because they would have seen that I was expecting and would not have given us the apartment.

My parents arrived at Alfonsas' parents'. We all managed to fit there for a few days, because we would be able to move only on the weekend. Old man Šiugžda had left a bed and a stove, so we were happy there would be a place to lie down. My parents moved with us to that apartment, because the landlords allowed them to stay there until they found a place of their own. Though there was not much room, it would suffice until my parents found their own apartment.

Not far away was a store owned by Lithuanians, the Lastauskas family. They gave us a kitchen table, a few chairs, and a bed for my parents. They also gave us some dishes, spoons, and a pot. So it was then good.

It was the middle of July and I could not do much. Mama took care of things and Ramutė watched. Tėtis and Stasys found jobs. Alfonsas worked in Newington, at Keeney Manufacturing. Though the work was hard we were happy that he was working.

The time finally came for me to go to the hospital. Because I had gained a lot of weight, the doctor scolded me and I had a very difficult labor. And after fourteen hours, a beautiful boy was born. Oh how happy we were that it was a boy and a healthy one. I stayed in the hospital for five days.

When I returned, I received a carriage to put the baby in. Ramutė's crib was already in our bedroom. Though there wasn't much space, it was good that I had my own room.

After about two weeks, the baby began to wheeze. I couldn't understand what was going on. When I picked him up in my arms, he seemed better. A few days later, after I nursed him, I put him into his carriage, thinking that he would fall asleep. He just laid there, eyes open, wheezing. Mama took one look at him and told me that my child could die and he wasn't even baptized yet. I called Elena Lastauskas and she came immediately. She made the sign of the cross over him and said that she was baptizing him with the name Jonas. She called the hospital and when we got there a priest was waiting because it appeared that the baby would die soon. Alfonsas and I both went with Elena. The priest immediately baptized him and they brought him to the children's ward. The priest told us that if the baby died, he would be baptized but if he lived then he would also have to be baptized in church.

That night was very difficult for me. I had to leave him. They put him into an oxygen tent. The next morning, after giving Ramutė breakfast, I went to the hospital. I found my baby in the oxygen tent, cold, connected to intravenous medicine. I was able to put my hand under the tent and touch him, but they would not let me pick him up and hold him. I was with him in the hospital every day. I often went there on foot because I didn't have ten cents for the bus. That's how eighteen days passed and they finally let him go home. By then I could no longer nurse him because I had to wean when he was in the hospital. The doctors told me that there had been nothing too dangerous and that he only had mucous in his lungs and that's why he had been wheezing. It then seemed as if everything was going well.

Alfonsas came home from work and said there was going to be a strike. And we needed so many things here. We had nothing we needed to live. Finally, the strike began. Alfonsas had to go walk in front of the factory carrying a placard. They gave strikers only twenty dollars a week. That was enough for food but how would we pay for everything else? We had no money saved. My parents paid the rent because they were living with us. Alfonsas' parents gave us fifty dollars and Vitas and Aldona gave us twenty. A bill arrived from the hospital for Jonas for more than five hundred dollars, though we had to pay only one hundred for my time in the hospital giving birth. I went to the hospital, told them our situation, so they gave us an extension and eventually we began to pay them five dollars a week.

 The strike dragged on for six weeks. Tėtis and Stasys were working, so Mama made food for us as well. That's how that time passed by. Alfonsas at last went back to work. Though he didn't earn much, we saved as much as we could. We were grateful for whatever we got from our older relatives or from other Lithuanians because we didn't have to buy it.

 Little Jonas was ten months old when I decided to go to work myself, at the North and Judd factory. They paid me seventy-five cents an hour and after a month raised it to eighty-five cents. It was good then. I earned almost twenty-five dollars a week. I worked for about six months. Mama was already tired out because the children were little and there was a lot of work with them. I decided not to go to work any longer. Ramutė didn't want to be without me and Little Jonas, my mother said, somehow fell off a chair and broke his arm. I saw that it was necessary for me to be at home. It was financially harder but children need their mother.

 I began not to feel well and discovered that I was expecting a little one again. Though we didn't plan it, but what can you do. My parents began to search for an apartment of their own because we needed more room. Alfonsas' brother Vitas with his family arrived from Chicago to move in with Alfonsas' parents. They would live in one apartment until they found something of their own. Well, I thought, lots of luck to them.

My parents were still not able to find an apartment of their own. Our landlords didn't want my parents living there with us any longer. Old man Šiugžda was very bad. He would not allow us even to have a telephone installed. I watched my children very carefully and never left them outside with him alone. I hid the fact that I was expecting another baby, because they did not want any children in their house. But so long as they didn't know that I was expecting a third, then for the time being it would be all right. But eventually I couldn't hide it any longer. My children were very good. They didn't run around the house. Finally, the time came for me to go to the hospital. It was August 9, 1952. After a long labor, a healthy boy was born, but I had wanted a girl. Alfonsas was very happy that there would be more men.

After five days, we returned home. There was so little space there but we had to fit another crib into our bedroom. There was no room so we put the crib in front of the closet door. If we needed to get something out, we would have to move the crib.

A month passed like this. Finally, my parents found an apartment in a house owned by Mrs. Pilkonis, on East Street, and so after almost three years we were alone. I was so happy that it was only my family living here now. We immediately bought beds for Ramutė and Little Jonas. The baby was in our bedroom. Though it wasn't easy, the children were small and we needed to buy many things, I did everything I could so we could manage.

We didn't have a car so we didn't go anywhere, there was no way to do that. The food stores weren't far so I carried groceries home. When my parents moved out they left me a washing machine. It was old, didn't work very well, but I was happy to have what I had. After a while, the machine broke, so I washed everything by hand. There was an old fashioned sink and I had a washboard, so I usually did laundry every day. Because the children were little, I didn't have to change their clothes often, and mostly had to wash the baby's diapers. There was no dryer, so I had to hang clothes out on a clothesline, winter and summer. We were used to it.

Mama would come to help, but it wasn't very often, because she had her own family. We stayed home mostly, out in the yard in the summer with the children. We didn't have a car so we had to stay in our own yard. On Sundays we would go to church, either I or Alfonsas, because the children were little. Eventually, we saved up enough money and bought a car, so it would be easier for Alfonsas to get to work and so we could go for rides on Sundays. Our greatest joy was to go what we called the „Ledų Farmukė" – the Ice Cream Farm – and eat ice cream. It was good to have a car, but it also needed to be repaired since it was old and broke down often.

We got together with our relatives – they at our home, we at theirs. Jonas, Alfonsas' brother, was married by then, so sometimes he and his wife Bronė would visit us. My parents would visit, Alfonsas' youngest brother Algis, my brother Stasys. It made passing time a bit more interesting.

The children were growing. Ramutė already had begun to go to kindergarten, Jonas played with Leonas. We were finally allowed to get a telephone, though it was quite an ordeal before they were able to run the line into our rooms. After putting the children to bed, I was so happy to have a chance to sit quietly and read.

It was cold in the apartment in the winter. There was no central heat and only a stove in the kitchen. We had to light the stove, and only in the evenings. It was a cast iron coal stove so it would cool over night and in the morning I had to clean out the ashes, fill it with fresh coal, and light it again. We heated water in a small tank, which I would light only when I had to bathe the children. It was fueled by gas.

We eventually bought a living room set, the first furniture we bought in America. What we had received from those old Lithuanians, a table, chairs, we kept because there was no money. We saved as much as we could because we did not know what would happen in the future.

In the spring I started to feel unwell. Well, once again, we were expecting a little one. Though there was much hardship, what could we do. It was hard for me because I had to wash everything by hand, we still didn't have a washing machine. Alfonsas worked long hours and I spent the days by myself with the children. It wasn't so bad in the summer, I could go sit outside. Fall was much harder. Little Leonas was still not able to walk and I had to wash his diapers by hand. I don't know how the time went by so quickly, but I was back in the hospital again. Mama barely managed to get to the house to look after the children when Alfonsas and I drove quickly to the hospital in New Britain. (We had already bought a different car.) A beautiful healthy boy was born quickly. That was November 23, 1953. I went home in five days. Mama helped for one more week and then I began to look after my family myself. Leonas wasn't walking yet and I had to carry both of them in my arms. Algirdas was a very good, calm baby, and while he slept a lot it was easier for me.

Leonas started to walk so I had to watch him all the time. Ramutė was in the first grade, and when she came home from school she would rock the little one. Down the hall was a little room – a porch – so it was good for me because even in the winter it was warm and the children mostly played there. The days passed monotonously. Housework, the children, and that was my whole life. My parents came to visit, stayed for a bit, and then left again. In the winter I mostly stayed at home, though occasionally Mama would come and I'd go to the store, to buy food at Abeciūnas' Market, and once in a while would go to church on Sunday, when Alfonsas would stay home with the children. Most important, the children were healthy and they had food to eat.

Shortly before Algirdas was born, Alfonsas began to work at Caval Tool machine shop. You had to work there for six months before you could qualify for health insurance, so once again we had to pay out of our own pockets. Little by little, we paid off the hospital. The children grew well, were healthy, though once in a while they'd catch colds but those passed quickly.

I didn't write down who the children's godparents were. Ramutė's were Alfonsas' brother Vitas and his wife Aldona; Jonas' were my brother Stasys and Elena (Helen) Lastauskas; Leonas' were Alfonsas' sister Onutė and his brother Jonas; and Algirdas' were Alfonsas' sister-in-law Bronė and his brother Algimantas (Algis).

Alfonsas' brother Algis was the one who visited us the most. He came over every Friday and brought chocolate for the children. Others came to visit as well but they came less often. That's how those days passed. The children grew and the work was always the same.

And 1955 came. Ramutė was in second grade and Jonas would go to kindergarten that fall.

April was a rainy month. Alfonsas had gone to church on Sunday. He talked with his brother Algis, who said he would be going to Hartford later that day with Vladas Plečkaitis, and he left his car at the church. That was the last time Alfonsas talked with him. About ten o'clock that night the telephone rang. Alfonsas' brother Jonas told Alfonsas that Algis and Vladas had had an automobile accident and that both were in the hospital. Alfonsas immediately went to the hospital and Jonas and Bronė were already there. The doctor came and handed Jonas a wallet, a watch, and said that he was very sorry but Algis had died. He had broken his neck. It was so horrible that someone so young, just twenty-two years old, had to die. Vladas was also injured but he was out of danger.

Alfonsas returned from the hospital, my parents arrived, and the two of us went to Alfonsas' parents.

That was April 24, 1955. I was so sad for him. It was very hard but we had to bear it all. The funeral services were beautiful, there were many people. Alfonsas suffered a great deal, but we had to leave all that behind as life continued to move forward.

In the fall, Jonas began to go to kindergarten. That first day was hard for him and for me. I was sad to leave him in kindergarten. He cried and wanted to go home. I left the room and watched hin through the window. After a little while, he calmed down and began to play with the other children. I picked him up after lunch. He said he liked it and the next day he went eagerly to kindergarten. He went to Smith School, which was not far from our house.

The children were growing well, Leonas was already running around the yard. Alfonsas' parents received insurance money after Algis' death and they gave each of their children one thousand dollars. We had already saved some money of our own, so Alfonsas' parents wanted us to buy a house together with them. I very much wanted to have my own house. Because here, old man Šiugžda was very bad and the children were very constrained.

We finally found a house at 26 Market Street in New Britain, a three family home. The previous owners lived on the first floor so that apartment was already available for us.

The rooms were large, there were three bedrooms, a big kitchen. I was so happy that we finally had our own house, though only half of it was actually ours, but it would be good for the children, no one would chase them away. Alfonsas' parents were supposed to go to the second floor but the people living there couldn't find a place to live and didn't move out. It was good for me. The children played, ran around, and were very content and happy. The school was nearby as well,

Chamberlain School. We bought the house on November 7, 1955. The winter passed well.

In the spring, my in-laws made a garden for themselves, though the yard was small, but the children could still play in it. Alfonsas' parents finally moved in to the second floor. My mother-in-law watched her gardens fom her window and, if the children threw a ball into her garden, she would get angry and yell at them. How could the children prevent that, they were still very young, and it was fun for them to run around in the yard. That's how the days passed, and sometimes I got angry because my mother-in-law was very hard to get along with. Alfonsas didn't concern himself with these things and never said anything to his mother. She mostly blamed me for everything.

I remember on Saturdays when Alfonsas went early to work and the children and I were still sleeping, she would begin to bang her little rugs against the wall, would begin pushing chairs around the kitchen so that none of us could sleep. Whenever I said anything to her, she replied that she had to take care of her house. It was very hard for me to live with her, but there was nothing I could do. I began to save money as much as I could. Once, because of her, I got so sick that I had to go to the hospital. I was very weak and could not eat. My doctor asked me what the matter was. I told him everything. He told me I shouldn't be living in the same house with her. But where could I go?

You will never know people until you live with them. Once I told Alfonsas' mother that my children had the right to play in their yard. She told me that if I wanted my little bastards to play then I should rent a park for them. I was very angered by that and told her that my children have a father, that she cannot call them bastards. Alfonsas, of course, didn't want to anger his mother, so he said nothing to her. I talked to my father-in-law, told him what was going on, and he told me there was nothing he could do, that that's how she is.

Sometimes Onutė's or Jonas' daughters would visit her. She would make pancakes for them and would lock her door so my children could not come in. Once, my children went upstairs to see their cousins, who were visiting. They were sitting at the kitchen table eating pancakes. When my children tried to open the screen door, it was locked and my mother-in-law told them to go away, that there was no food for them here. Or when my children were playing with their cousins and the ice cream truck came, my mother-in-law would buy ice cream for the girls and, though my children wanted ice cream, too, there was nothing for them. I would wait for the ice cream truck too, and when it came back I'd by ice cream for my children.

That's how the days passed. I had to endure a great deal and will not write everything down here. She did blame me for many things. She accused me of stealing her statue of Mary, said that I had broken off the heads of her plastic flamingos in the yard. My brother Stasys had given me that statue of Mary when we moved into this house and it stood outside in the yard near the bushes. Things got even worse when my parents moved into the third floor. That was a big mistake.

Across the street from us lived an old single woman, a widow, and she liked me very much. She was hard of hearing but we were able to converse. Mrs.Berg was her last name. She noticed how hard it was for my children in their own yard. She called me over once and told me that her neighbor in the back, Mrs.Moorcroft, was selling her house. It was a two-story house with a lot of land, three bedrooms. It was an old and slightly crooked house. But she told me to go and take a look. You might be able to buy it, she told me, there will be more room for your children and no one will yell at them.

I immediately went to see Mrs. Moorcroft. She was a very pleasant woman. We talked a lot and she told me she knew about my life from her neighbor and that she would sell me the house. I was very happy. I told Alfonsas when I got home. I said that if we needed help, my parents could lend us money. The price of the house was nineteen thousand dollars and we had saved only two thousand. We had to make a down payment of six thousand dollars. My parents lent us four thousand. We got a mortgage from the bank, and I was overjoyed that we would at last have a place all our own.

But there were people among us who, when they learned that we were buying the house, offered Mrs. Moorcroft two thousand dollars more so she would sell the house to them. When I went to see her one day, Mrs. Moorcroft told me that my sister-in-law, Zita Dreslius, my brother Stasys' wife, had come to her and offered her more money. But she told me that she told my sister-in-law that she had promised the house to me and would sell it only to me. I was very distressed that my brother's wife wanted to do such a thing to us, going behind my back like that. But Mrs. Moorcroft liked me and said that it would be good for my children there.

We inspected the house. The first floor had been updated, there was a sunroom added in the back. The second floor was old, the bathroom old, there were very few closets. There was a two-car garage, and on the side of the garage was a new room, recently built, where the children could play. But it looked like a palace to me. There were many trees and spruces, grapevines, the yard was very big, and though there would be much work, it would be ours alone.

Finally, on August 29, 1962, we moved to our own place. We rented our first floor apartment to a single man, Benny Birenbaum, and he paid us eighty dollars a month. That was good because we paid forty dollars for our share of the monthly payment for the three family house and still had forty left over for our new home. Alfonsas' parents insisted that we give them half the rent from our first floor apartment, even though we still owned the house together, but I said no. It was still our part of the house, and they were already collecting the rent from the third floor and were living in their apartment for free. Alfonsas' brothers agreed with their mother's demands, and Alfonsas was ready to do that, but I told Alfonsas to tell them that it was our part of the house and we would not pay them for what was ours.

There was much work in the new house. But it wasn't hard because it was our house. Whatever the children wanted to do, they could do. There was a lot of room everywhere. While it was still warm outside, we took care of the yard. There were many dead bushes, trees, dried branches, and we burned everything that we trimmed. Though we were left with no money and there were many repairs to be made, we fixed what we could when we could. The children and their friends spent much time in the room alongside the garage, it was their place. When the children all went off to school, and Alfonsas to work, I spent most of my time working outside. It was delightful to do that work because this was our first home.

The children grew well, studied well. Ramutė was finishing high school and was getting ready to go to college, to Annhurst College near Putnam. I always thought that I never wanted my children to work in factories. That was in 1965. When my daughter finished high school, I knew that it would be difficult for us to live on one income and send her to college, so I started to work at Stamping & Bending Co. in New Britain. It wasn't far from home. Though it was hard – working in the factory, taking care of the house, getting the children off to school – but I had to work, from 7:30 in the morning until 5:00 o'clock in the evening. I got a half hour for lunch, so I would run home at noon, make lunch for Alfonsas, who came home from the factory from noon to 1:00 o'clock, and then I'd run back to punch the clock at 12:30 again.

Jonas worked one summer, when he was turning fourteen, with my brother Stasys, on his knees banging nails into the floor of a house Stasys was adding a room to. He also worked for Stasys when he was building an apartment house on land we sold to him. Jonas was paid one dollar an hour.

Leonas and Algirdas used to deliver newspapers six days each week. So all three of my boys were trying to earn some money for themseves. In the summer of 1966, Jonas was chosen to go to Yale Summer High School. He was a good sudent. He was there at Yale for six weeks and didn't work for my brother any more.

Ramutė was getting ready to go to Annhurst College in the fall of 1965. I had gotten my first wages and I bought everything for her that she needed. I used to sew clothes for her, too. And then the time came for my daughter to move to Putnam. I was so happy that she was going to further her education. Though it wasn't easy for me to work and take care of the house and my family, I knew that it would be better for my children.

In the fall, the children went back to school. I no longer had to worry about what they would be doing all day long when I was at work. I would make supper when I came home from work. Leonas and Algirdas came home from school at about three o'clock so they were at home without me until I came back, at around five o'clock. Jonas was busy at the high school and would come home later.

It was hard for me because I didn't have a dryer, so winter and summer I had to hang the laundry outside, and there was a lot of laundry. On Saturdays, I would clean the house, do laundry, and the whole day would pass. On Sundays we went to church, then had Sunday dinner, and a few hours of rest, and then I had to get ready to go back to work again the next morning. I did everything I could to make sure that my children were well taken care of. And once a month we would drive up to Putnam to visit Ramutė.

In September 1967 my brother Pranas and his family came to visit us from Germany. We had not seen each other since July 1949. Their children, Norbert and Brigita, stayed with us every day and so did Pranas and Emma (though they slept at my parents'), so every day when I came home from work I had to make supper for everyone. They stayed with us for four weeks.

Ramutė had finished two years at Annhurst College, and that summer we knew that she would be going to study in Mexico, at the University of the Americas in Puebla, because she had won a Spanish language competition that year. Though it was sad to think that she would be so far away, we knew that it would be good for her.

Tėtis was already sick. Though he tried to continue working in the factory, he couldn't go on for long. We had to take him to see doctors, to the hopsital, so I did what I could to be of help to him. Stasys also was not well, he drank far too much, so there was no help from him. He didn't take care of his car and it broke down. He took Tėtis's car and that woman he lived with crashed it. Though Stasys had been married and had a daughter, because of his drinking everything in his life unraveled. I won't write about that, because I had to endure many things. He began to live with Eva. She also liked to drink, and that's how their life turned out. His life could have been a very good one, because he was quite talented and had good hands – everything he took on he could do well – but because of his drinking everything perished, even his health. He didn't work anywhere, he was supported on welfare together with his „wife."

We let Ramutė off to Mexico, and how hard it was for me. I worked in the factory and would send her as much money as I could manage. She came home for Christmas. That's how the winter passed.

Jonas graduated from high school and received a full scholarship to Yale University. We were overjoyed. He had graduated from high school at the top of his class, he was a good student, and so they valued his talents. Even though it was hard for me, but I was so happy that my children were doing well. That makes everything lighter. In the summer, the children had jobs so they were at least able to earn a little money for themselves.

In the fall of 1968 Ramutė went back to Mexico and Jonas went to Yale. I was so happy that my children were on a good road. Though it was very difficult for me to let my daughter go so far away, I still knew that my girl was on the right path and that the year would pass quickly. Though there were some unpleasant events when she was there, especially when she was robbed in Mexico City of everything she had brought from home. It was good from the perspective that her suitcases had been in an American Embassy car and our insurance paid us for most of her losses.

Jonas was doing well at Yale and we would go to visit him. Leonas and Algirdas were in high school, so there was less work for me. Winter passed, spring came. Jonas finished his first year at Yale. Alfonsas and I talked often that we needed to do something so we wouldn't have to spend the rest of our lives working in factories. Though we worked hard, there wasn't much money to show for it. One day, at the end of April 1969, the two of us didn't go to work and instead we drove up and down the Berlin Turnpike, stopping at every motel along the way, and I went in to ask if they might be selling it.

And we got to the Maple Motel. I went into the office and asked if they might be selling. The owner wasn't there, just her assistant. She said that Mrs. Menard was thinking about selling and that she would be back on Saturday.

The place looked not too bad and we returned on Saturday. The owner was a very pleasant woman. We talked a lot with her, and she finally agreed to sell us the motel for $127,000. Alfonsas and I thought a great deal about how we would do all of the necessary work. I was only forty-one years old and I was not afraid of hard work. That's because I didn't know what that work would, in fact, be for me. And we put our house up for sale. Alfonsas' parents bought our half of the three-family house we had bought with them. A few weeks later, a buyer for our house also appeared.

We agreed that we would take the motel over on May 30, 1969. It was a lot of work for me to pack up the house. I was no longer going to work at the factory. We signed the papers to sell our house.

We moved to the motel on May 29, 1969. It was a new place and I knew nothing about running a motel. There wasn't much space for us. Mrs. Menard showed me how to answer the telephone, manage the office, register guests, and so on. And a few days later, I was on my own. Alfonsas was still working in the factory because he didn't yet want to leave his job and we also had health insurance from his factory.

It was hardest for me because Friendly Acres Motel was also on the same switchboard as our motel, so there were a great many calls and I still had to clean the rooms. Everything was quite neglected. There was a great deal of work to be done and the rooms were in need of much care. There were four rooms with kitchenettes, and they were so dirty because it seems no one before had cleaned them very well. And people were coming to rent rooms. I hurried to clean because I also had to take care of the office. It was easier when the children came back for the summer because they would help me with the telephone. And besides that, Tėtis was very sick, so I had to look after him and take him to the doctor. And even more, I needed an operation, a hysterectomy. It was good that Ramutė came home from Mexico. But there was nothing else to do, so I went into the hospital and was there for five days after surgery.

The childen were running the motel. It was July 1969. I returned from the hospital and, after a week, I was doing all of my jobs again. We brought my father to the motel to see how we were living. He was so sad that he couldn't do any work, and there was a lot he could have helped us with. He stayed for a little while and then went home. From then on, he spent most of his time in bed.

Ramutė was working through the summer as was Jonas. They were earning some money for themselves. There was very little room for the children in the apartment where we lived in the motel. There were too few rooms. The motel was doing pretty well. We paid all of our bills and there was money left over for ourselves. We got along very well with the former owner, Mrs. Menard. She suggested that we build a house. She said there would be more room and that the three rooms we were now occupying for ourselves could be rented and they would cover the building costs. We were considering what to do. Though we didn't have too much money, we decided that, to make things better for the family, we needed to build a house. We went to the bank and increased our mortgage. We borrowed fifteen thousand dollars. And we began to build the house.

I heard that there was a woman in New Britain who could tell the future using cards. We both went. She laid out the cards for me and said that I had just been somewhere taking care of paperwork. She said that we wanted to do something at home and added that when we begin the work we would find a large rock on the right side. But we would overcome that and the work would continue. She said that we would live well, there would be a lot of work, but everything would be for the good.

Well, we decided to start building and they came to dig the foundation. They dug in a few places, all was well, but when they began to dig on the right side, they said they found a huge rock and they could not continue to dig. We hired people with a machine capable of breaking up the rock because it wasn't possible to use explosives there. It was too close to other buildings. It cost us dearly until that machine crumbled that rock and they could begin to pour the new foundation for the house.

It was hard for me when I had to do everything at the motel. Alfonsas took a vacation from the factory to look after the building of the house. But there were many other worries. Tėtis was not able to get out of bed and I had to help Mama also. The motel was mostly full all the time. We had many workers who stayed for five days and went home on Fridays. That was good profit. I understood everything about the motel by then and knew what needed to be done. The building of the house was going well and Alfonsas extended his vacation from the factory. Though the factory bosses weren't happy, they allowed him the extension.

Autumn came quickly. The children went back to school. Tėtis, by then, was getting worse. He could not go to the doctors very much and I no longer brought him to the hospital because there was no help they could give him. Mama looked after him and I helped her as much as I could. At the end of October, Stasys came to stay with our parents. Alfonsas and I also went. Tėtis was mostly unconscious, and a little after nine in the evening, on October 27, 1970, he died.

There were many worries with the funeral, but we made all of the arrangements and the services concluded well. Mama remained living in that same place, though no one else lived there, and she managed well on her own. I would bring her to my home, she would stay with us for a little while, and then would want to go home again to her own place.

Our house was already finished and we could move in. There was more room for us and for the children. I was happy that everything seemed to be going well.

Ramutė that summer began to work as a travel agent and met Robert Mills. We very much had wanted that she meet someone who was Lithuanian and a Catholic, but this was her choice and we didn't interfere. We were able to celebrate Christmas in the new house. We rented out the three rooms we had been living in and the rent paid for our new house payment. Everything was going well, though there was a great deal of work for me. Alfonsas was still working in the factory. I had to clean the rooms, take care of the office, and do all sorts of other jobs. It became too much for me. I told Alfonsas that he should quit his job at the factory and that the two of us would work at the motel. He always thought that if something didn't go well at the motel, he would at least have his factory job. But he finally saw that the business was going quite well, so in February 1971 he came home from work one day with his tools and said he would no longer be going to the factory. That would be good for me because now there would be two of us and it would be easier for me with all of the motel work. I had to check people in, pay the bills, manage the accounts, prepare the books and taxes. In the evenings, I worked mostly in the office. Even though, when we bought the motel, I had known nothing about that business, I learned it quickly. I liked that work.

Mama had to move out of the house where she was living because the owners sold it. We gave Mama a room at the end of the motel, near the highway. She was content at first and would come to me, would walk around the motel, helped me with the laundry. Mama very much wanted to talk but I didn't even have time to sit down. The telephones would ring, people would come to the office, the rooms needed to be cleaned, I had my family to look after, and I had to cook and do laundry for them as well. Mama began to get restless, would say she had no one to talk to. But I was so busy that I didn't have even an hour for myself. In the spring, there was a great deal of work to do in the yard. Alfonsas took care of a lot of things himself because various things would break.

Ramutė began to date Robert seriously. Leonas had been dating Marytė Maurutytė for some time. We knew her parents back in the camps in Germany. Jonas also had a girlfriend named Susan. They would come to visit us and would stay for a few days. Leonas was going to St. Michael's College in Vermont. Everyone was studying well and would come home in the summers, so it was easier for me, too, because they would help with the office.

There were seventeen rooms and they all required much work every day. It was hard for me. Alfonsas would help with the cleaning but there was work to be done in the yard, too, so I had a great deal to do.

One day, Ramutė told us that she and Robert were planning to have a wedding. And so there were more worries to plan the wedding. But everything was arranged well and on August 5, 1972, we had a wedding. My Aunt Olga with my cousin Kirsten came. Alfonsas' cousin Romas with his family flew in from Chicago. Everyone stayed at the motel. There was a lot of work at the motel and here was the wedding and guests, and I had to make meals for them all as well. Even though our relatives knew that there was a lot of work for us, not one of them helped us. Vitas and his wife had a motel, they could have taken Romas and his family in, but they didn't do that.

The wedding was right at hand, everyone looked good. Alfonsas' cousin Antanas Vaitkus and his wife Marion also arrived, but they stayed with Alfonsas' brother Jonas because we had no room.

It was sad to give my daughter away. Alfonsas led her to the altar. Everything was beautiful in church, the reception hall was beautifully set up, the dinner was delicious, there were many people, Radionovas' orchestra played wonderfully, and everyone was happy. The wedding passed well and the two of them traveled to Hawaii for their honeymoon.

Romas and his family, and Aunt Olga and Kirsten, stayed with us for a week. Every wedding has its worries until all is arranged and until everything passes. But it seems that all was good, that all went well, and finally we were able to concern ourselves only with our motel. Our guests left, so it was easier for me because I didn't have to prepare all that food every day.

Ramutė and Robert returned and settled into their apartment. Once again, everything began to flow along its own path. There was a lot of work in the motel, we were doing well financially. I could write a lot about all of this, but it doesn't make sense to do so, because it was all too much for me sometimes, and I thought that I would not be able to manage it all.

Mama no longer wanted to live with us. She found herself an apartment in New Britain, in housing designed only for elderly people, and we moved her there. Stasys would come from Waterbury to visit Mama. He would stay for a day or so and, having gotten money from her, would go back again. He drank a lot whenever he got money, and that was his bad side. Though I begged him often, yelled at him, nothing helped with his drinking. He had spent time in the hospital and that hadn't helped either. That was his destiny. He could have worked at the motel more, as well, but after a couple of days he had had enough.

Jonas had graduated from Yale and had received a fellowship to continue his studies for a doctoral degree, a Ph.D. We were so happy that our children were doing so well in their studies. It was my greatest joy that my dreams were being fulfilled and my children were beginning to stand well on their own feet.

In the fall, Jonas went to graduate school. Everything seemed to be going well in our family. Ramutė and Robert bought a house in Glastonbury and we were so happy that they would be living not too far away. They lived in that house for less than a year because Robert was offered a job in Rochester, New York. It was very sad that they were going to be moving so far away, but it was not according to our will. They moved to Fairport, where they bought a house. Ramutė got a job teaching Spanish. Algirdas had graduated from high school and was going on to Hartford Community College and then, later, to Central Connecticut State University. We were working together in the motel, and everything was going well.

Leonas and Marytė told us that they were planning to get married. Once again it fell on us to arrange a wedding, because Marytė's mother lived in Vermont and her father in Waterbury. Her father helped with the wedding but her mother didn't even come. On September 27, 1975, we had the wedding, in the same place that Ramutė and Robert held their reception.

This wedding passed as well and the two of them lived in their own apartment. Leonas had a good job and Marytė started to go to Central Connecticut State University, wanting to get her diploma and to become a teacher.

That's how 1976 arrived. We learned that Ramutė was expecting her first baby and we rejoiced that we would be grandparents. And on February 23, 1976, she had a son, Biliukas. We were very happy that the birth went well and after a couple of days we went to visit Ramutė. He was a beautiful boy. It was so wonderful to hold my grandson in my arms. I stayed at Ramutė's because she needed help after she returned from the hospital. I helped her for only a week. She got stronger and I had to go back to take care of the motel. I flew back. It was the first time in my life that I flew in an airplane. Alfonsas had been taking care of the motel and had some help.

Once again, in our wider family, there was another misfortune. On May 20, Rymis (Vitas' son) died by his own hand. What happened to him that he, being so young, only twenty-two years old, did not want to live. Vitas and his family suffered terribly through all that. We all did.

The days passed well. We had some savings. Everything was good and we were happy that we were at last in good standing. Though there was a great deal of work, every day cleaning the rooms, seven days a week. Even at night there was little rest. The telephone would ring, people would come to ask for rooms. I had to get up even at night, because Alfonsas would never get up.

We decided to go for a few weeks to Germany to visit Pranas. The children told us to go. Jonas took care of the motel, Algirdas helped him, and we had a woman who came to help clean the rooms. So in the summer of 1977 we went to Germany for three weeks. It was our first vacation in eight years. It was good to spend time with Pranas, to see all those places where we lived when we were first married. We visited my brother Povilas, too. And we returned home. Back to that same work again. I won't write about all of the details, because it was my daily work. I had a woman who would come to help clean rooms, so it was a little easier for me.

And we had a second grandchild. Ramutė and Robert had a son Davukas, who was born June 4, 1979.

The children would come to visit, friends, relatives, and that's how our days ran past. Jonas became acquainted with Genutė Stankaitytė and they began to see each other. When he finished his studies, he received his Ph.D. He had not yet found a job but eventually found one teaching and writing in a big company and it appeared that they were serious in their relationship. I encouraged him to marry her and, eventually, he told us that they would be getting married. We didn't have to do much for that wedding because the Skankaitis family took care of it, and on October 6, 1979, there was a wedding. Everything went well. My mother and Alfonsas' parents both also were able to go. We were happy that everything had gone well and that the children seemed to be happy. Jonas and Genutė had their own apartment and began to live.

Alfonsas' father was already not feeling well. He had lung cancer. But he was still managing pretty well. We would go to visit them. They were already living in West Hartford. My father-in-law kept getting worse, though the doctors treated him the best they could as the cancer progressed. Alfonsas' father continued to decline and in mid-November 1980, he died. The funeral passed as all such funerals do, and it was quite sad.

My mother got sick in October and I took her to the hospital. She need her gall bladder removed. They didn't operate on her and she got an infection of her gall bladder. By the time they did the surgery, it was too late. The infection had spread everywere. She did not come home. She spent five weeks in the hospital and was later transferred to a nursing home.

It was hard for me because every day I went to look after my mother, and there was all the work to finish at the motel, and that's how five weeks passed. Stasys came to visit Mama only once. By then she didn't recognize him. Mama died on December 3, 1980. And once again a funeral, with everything on our shoulders. Stasys didn't help at all. He did not even come to the funeral. My brothers did not come from Germany either. We did everything with our children and buried her beautifully.

During Christmas we went to Waterbury. I wanted to give Stasys something at least for the holidays. We had to wait a long time until we were allowed to go into his apartment. But we visited with him for a time. Alfonsas gave him some money and I brought food, and so on. So they might have a better holiday because they were living on welfare.

Alfonsas' mother lived alone in that apartment and later she was given a smaller one. Her sons visited her every day, looked after her. Though it was difficult for me because I had to take care of the motel alone, but what could I have said? It was his mother, and twice a week it was his turn to go visit her.

That's how time ran past. In March 1981 we decided to go to Florida for a week with our friends the Skopases. The children let us go. I was happy that we would have a good rest. Before leaving, Alfonsas wanted to take care of the lights on the motel roof. When he was climbing down, the ladder slipped and Alfonsas fell from the roof. It was good that I was home. Algirdas had just gotten back from work and was sleeping. The ambulance arrived immediately and took him to the hospital and I went in the ambulance with him. He broke his leg at the ankle and needed surgery. He was in the hospital for a week. I was left to clean the motel by myself and to take care of all the other tasks. My helper didn't come back and I was left alone. There was a great deal to be done and Algirdas helped as much as he could. The motel was always full and I cleaned rooms from early morning until late in the afternoon. In the evenings Algirdas watched the office and I went to the hospital to see Alfonsas. When he returned from the hospital, he could not be of much help, though he was able to sit in the office. His leg was in a cast for a long time. That's how the time passed. After two months, he was able to walk fully again.

My cleaning lady came back, though I was angry at her for having abandoned me at the time when I needed help the most. But I took her back because I could not find anyone else who didn't want to work full time. She worked four days a week. That was fine because the most work was from Friday until Monday. On Sundays, either Alfonsas or I would go to church in New Britain. We couldn't go to very many places because the children were living on their own, had their own houses, so there was work to be done there by them on weekends as well. Algirdas was working full-time with the police. So he had to rest as much as he could, too, because he worked mostly nights, and in the motel, when people came to the office, the bell rang in our apartment, too, and it was harder for him to rest during the day.

That's how the days passed. Life in the motel brought nothing new. There was a lot of work, our income was good. The children came to visit us to help. Stasys would come to help with some things as well, but his health was not very good. He drank too much though he had been forbidden to do so.

In the summer, in 1982, we welcomed a granddaughter. She was born on July first, a beautiful girl, my son Jonas' and his wife Genutė's daughter, named Kristina. We now had three grandchildren. We were so happy with our children's good fortune. We were also waiting for another grandchild. My son Leonas and his wife Marytė were expecting the birth of a new little one.

Summer passed and fall arrived with its beauties. Work was the same, we were doing well financially, our income was good. On December 16, 1982, we welcomed our fourth grandchild. Leonas and Marytė had a son, Levukas. He was a beautiful child, and though he was not very big when he was born, he was growing perfectly.

Christmas passed wonderfully. All the children were with us. We greeted the new year of 1983. In March, my brother Pranas called to say that he was coming from Germany to visit us. We were looking forward to seeing them. They arrived at the end of May. It was wonderful to see him. Though we could not take them very far, our relatives and friends welcomed them pleasantly and those three weeks went by quickly.

Summer was coming to its close. On August 20, Stasys called me. We talked for a long time. I asked about his health, he said he was going to see a doctor because he wasn't feeling well. Stasys asked me what I wanted to do with that place in the cemetery, where our parents had a spot for him. I told him, Stasys, that place is yours and if you go there or not that was our parents' desire because your name is on the gravestone. So he said to me, Then bury me there. We talked a lot about our lives. That was on Saturday. On Monday I mailed him some money. Then on Saturday, August 27, 1983, in the morning, the telephone rang and a man's voice asked for me. He said, Your brother Stasys died last night. It was such an awful feeling, that my brother was gone.

We drove to Waterbury, Alfonsas and I, Leonas, and Stasys' daughter Zina. How hard it was to see my dead brother lying there. We made arangements with the funeral home. They brought him to New Britan. Alfonsas and I took care of everything necessary so the funeral would a good one. Our sons helped a great deal. Everything went well. We buried him alongside my parents. Though his „wife" didn't want him to be buried here, there was nothing she could do because that was his desire. I called my brother in Germany to tell him that Stasys had died. Pranas could not come and Povilas wasn't feeling well and did not have the money for the trip. We took care of everything without them.

Everything went back to the same routine. That work began to be too hard for me. I no longer wanted to work as much. We began to think about selling the motel. Though we had kept the motel for many years, the time had come, I was tired. We began to look around for a house to buy. We were not in a hurry, saw many houses, though I wanted to stay here in Newington, because it was not far from church and everything else was familiar.

Finally, after having seen many houses, we found a small house for ourselves. We liked the surrounding neighborhood, the house wasn't bad, and was in a good location. We bought it and Algirdas moved in immediately to live in the house. We were left in the motel alone. When Algirdas was still living with us, we could at least leave for a couple of hours now and then, for our own needs. But not now. And Alfonsas still went to see his mother a few times a week. And I needed to be by myself in the motel and in the office. But what could I do, I had to look after everything.

We bought the house in May 1984. Alfonsas put a lot of work into the house because there was much to change to make it what we wanted it to be. Albinas Petkaitis also did a lot of work there. Alfonsas helped me at the motel and then went to the house to make renovations. I also went there because it needed a good cleaning. Algirdas was working, and living in the house was good for him because he was able to sleep when he came home from work. Algirdas took care of himself and there wasn't much for me to do for him.

My cleaning lady at the motel stopped coming to work and moved to East Hartford. I was left to clean all the rooms on my own and to take care of all the other jobs. I began to get very tired and thought that it was time for me to rest. And autumn was here and there were more jobs outside in the yard as well. Winter arrived and there was a lot of snow, and we had to work a long time to clean it all out. Algirdas also came to help. We began to think seriously about selling.

Then Indians began looking to buy motels. Many of them came through and we chose a young family and agreed to sell them the motel on July 1, 1985. It was good that we made that decision because work needed to be done and things needed to be modernized. Our telephones, for example, were still put through a switchboard in the office and people began to want to call out from their rooms on their own. In addition, the rooms were in need of additional renovation, much remained to be done, and the heating system wasn't the best and the air conditioners were old. If we had decided to stay longer in the motel, then it would have been worth it to put money into that work, but we already wanted to leave and so did no more renovations. But our buyer came, looked around, and was satsified with everything.

The day we sold the motel finally came. I cleaned the rooms in the morning because I wanted to leave everything clean, and in the afternoon we signed the papers and drove to our house.

How strange it was for me that, after so many years, the telephones were not ringing, the doorbells were not chiming. I seemed to be lost, didn't know what to do with myself. I began to think we had made a mistake by selling the motel.

But after a time I began to get used to it. We took care of the house, looked for furniture. We thought about going to Chicago to see Alfonsas' cousin Romas and to visit my aunt in

Milwaukee. That's how we ended up in Chicago and, having stayed a few days with Romas and his wife Nijolė, we went to visit my relatives. Though I had not seen Aunt Greta in many years, they welcomed us nicely, but her daughters, though they were my cousins, were strangers to me. We visited another aunt also, Lida, and her family, and went to visit my cousin Rita also. We stayed a few days and then returned to Chicago. I would have gone home right then, but our tickets would be good only in a week so we had to stay with them. I felt as if I was not in my own place and did not want to burden them. Well, we finally came home and our life without work began.

My former sister-in-law, Zita, was sick. She was in the hospital in Boston. She needed a new liver because hers was not functioning. Time passed and they operated on her, giving her a new liver. We would go to visit her.

There wasn't much to do so we took care of the house and the yard. I would go to the motel to pick up their monthly payment check. It was somehow sad. Everything had once been ours and now others were walking around our place. Everything changes.

And we had another grandchild, our fifth. Jonas' and Genutė's daughter, Joanna, was born on March 27, 1985.

Then the New Year, 1986, arrived. We decided to go to Florida with Jonas Jonynas and his wife Angelė. We left in the beginning of February in their car. We stopped at their daughter's, spent the night, and drove on. The trip was fine, though it was sometimes boring, too. At times I regretted that I went. In Florida we visited friends, went to Disney World. The trip home was the same.

When we got home, everything was the same as it had been. It was good to spend the summer at home. I began to get used to not having anything I needed to do. Taking care of the yard and house was the same. Our everyday life was going well and I can't write it all down because there was nothing of much interest going on.

Perhaps sometimes I don't know how to be happy with what life gives to me. And there are so many happy hours and sad ones. We went everywhere we could, to events, to visit friends and acquaintances, and time passed quickly.

And there were hard days, too. We were deeply saddened when Marytė lost a baby in 1985. She wasn't able to carry it to full term, and the baby was born prematurely. I suppose it's what was meant to be. They already had a child who was growing well. A year later, she suffered the same kind of event. That was in 1986. She lost two girls, twins. I was with her at the hospital, and because she gave birth prematurely, the two of them did not live long. I held them in my arms. They were so tiny and I was overwhelmed with sadness for them. My son Leonas baptised them both and after a short time they left us. It was so hard to see my children suffer. In 1988, Marytė gave birth to a beautiful girl, Jessica. She was under the care of good doctors and everything went successfully. We were so happy that we had six grandchildren, all of them healthy and growing well.

Alfonsas had begun to sing in a quartet when we were still in the motel. He was going to rehearsals still and I thought he would continue to do so because he likes songs and loves to sing. There were times when they were invited to sing somewhere farther away and I would go, too.

My son Leonas and Marytė wanted to have a bigger house and they found some land they liked. They started building a house for them. They were farther away, but they liked it there.

We decided that, after so many years, it was time for us to go to Lithuania. It was our dream to see those places where we were born, grew up, spent our childhoods. We began to get ready for our journey. There were many things we needed to arrange, because in those days it was still necessary to travel through Moscow. Leonas and Marytė sold their house and came to live with us for a few weeks. And we left a week later.

We flew on Austrian Airlines, and in New York we met a group of Lithuanians who would be traveling on the same plane to Lithuania. We knew them, so the trip to Moscow was fine.

We had to pass through control points in Moscow, and it was very dirty there, people were not smiling, had icy faces. They took us by bus to a different airport. We ate there and got on the plane to Vilnius. They were speaking in Lithuanian on the plane. We waited a long time to take off. There was no air conditioning on the plane and it was so hot that I thought I would not be able to endure it. We finally began to move and the air cooled off. It was not a big plane and when we finally reached Vilnius it was already dark. My cousin Jonas and my cousin Marytė's son Ričardas were at the airport waiting for us. We had to go through passport control once again. We finally picked up our bags and drove by car to Kaunas. Though it was night, I kept looking out the windows and could not believe that we were really in Lithuania. Jonas' and Ričardas' families were waiting for us when we got to Ričardas' home. It was so wonderful to see them all. We talked until early morning, slept until noon. I could not believe that, after forty-eight years, I was here once again.

We traveled to many places, but we mostly visited those places where we had spent our childhoods. I had many memories, but seeing those places I could not believe that they were the same. Everything had changed, many buildings had been built, those places where there were beaches and forests were now part of the city. There were no people left that I knew in my childhood. We traveled to Pažaislis, where I walked so many times when I was a girl. There had been a beautiful church there, a convent, but now I was speechless when I saw what the Russians had done. It was neglected and rundown, the outside walls had been knocked down, there were holes in the church walls, there was no altar. The convent, which had been so beautiful, was crumbling. It had been converted by the Russians into an insane asylum. It was horrifying to see.

I was so sad for those places which, in my eyes, had been so wonderful then. They said that now that they had formed a new Lithuanian government, they would begin to rebuild the church and the convent.

The houses where I had lived no longer existed. Even those locations themselves had changed. There were new buildings everywhere. Where we had bathed in the Nemunas as children and where there had been meadows, now were embankments filled with rocks, cement, and all sorts of trash. The doors of the church where we would go to mass on Sundays were closed and locked. We could not go inside. People I stopped to talk to about those places, to ask them if they could tell me anything about them, would not say much and were very unfriendly, looked at us with deep suspicion. I missed those places where my childhood had run past.

In Kaunas we stayed with Ričardas and his wife Juta. We took walks through Kaunas. We visited my cousin Marytė (Ričardas' mother), but she was in bed, was ill. It was very good to see her after so many years. She had been raised by my mother and had lived with us until she was sixteen years old because her mother had remarried and the new husband did not want to take care of Marytė. I spent a great deal of time with her. I was sad that she thought that she would get better, but destiny had a different fate for her. I was very happy to see another one of my cousins, Genė. Though I didn't spend much time with her, because she lived far away, and I didn't have a chance to go to her home.

In Kaunas there were still many Russian soldiers, but the Lithuanians had already begun changing the names of streets back to what they had been called before the Russians came. They took us to the Hill of Crosses in Šiauliai. It was truly impressive for me to see that hill. There were so many crosses that it was hard to imagine that such a place in fact existed.

Everything was as if in a dream, because after so many years I once again saw the land where I was born. It was just sad that my childhood girl friends were not there. I so much wanted to see them and to talk with them about our long-passed youth. We also went to Palanga, near the Baltic Sea. There were amazing sunsets there. It was just unfortunate that our room did not have its own bathroom and we had to share that facility with others.

We also traveled to Vilnius. It is a beautiful city, though many places there had been neglected, but we could see that they were then starting to renovate some buildings. We visited Castle Hill, museums, theaters, walked through many shops, though there was nothing good to buy there.

Those four weeks passed by so quickly and then it was time to go home. And once again through Moscow on the way back. And how dirty and unfriendly those people were. They checked our passports, documents, and luggage over and over. Finally, they let us over to the Austrian side. My eyes brightened when I saw how clean it was, how friendly the people were, how pleasantly they served us. When we at last arrived in Vienna, we went to the hotel because our plane for home would be leaving only the next day. The hotel was very nice, clean, we ate dinner in a fine restaurant, looked around the city.

The time passed well and after breakfast we began to get ready to go to the airport. The trip home went well, our children were waiting for us in New York. It was good to be in my own home, to lie down in my own bed. We talk often with one another about the time we had spent in the land where we were born.

August 2007

We have been to Lithuania three times. Our time there passed well each visit. We also have been to Germany three times to visit Pranas, the last time in 1993. Pranas came to visit us five times, because after Emma died he had time and he was very happy to spend it with us.

I'm no longer thinking about any other trips out of the country because I'm not so young any more and have pain in my joints. I don't want to take any more long journeys, because each one is exhausting, especially for me. It's comfortable to travel by car and I'm very happy to do so, especially when we go to visit our daughter, because her home is like a second home to me. And to see my great-granddaughters, they are lovely girls. We are so happy that we have lived long enough to have great-granddaughters.

* * *

We have reached the sixtieth anniversary of our life together. When you think about it, we have been together a very long time. Though, in reality, we have already been together for sixty-two years. When I sometimes remember those days of our youth, how beautiful everything was, even though we didn't have much, I think about how those years passed by so quickly and how all that remain are pleasant memories.

We live quietly now. We don't need much. We see the children and their families, they visit us. Jonas stops by frequently on his way home from work to visit. It is wonderful when all the children come togeher, there is so much happiness and laughter when they remember their younger days.

Alfonsas doesn't sing much any more now. If they invite him to come sing at church he always goes, but his concerts have ended now because they are no longer young and there are younger ones who perform. But we are content with our life. We go to where we need to go and relatives and friends come to visit us, so they sing together, we laugh, the time passes well.

At Christmas, the family gathers at our home. It is a wonderful time, seeing everyone together. Though it's sad that Ramutė and her family live so far away and can't participate in that family gathering. But I always feel as if they are all with us, at least in my thoughts. I miss them very much because we don't see each other often.
In the fall we went to visit them, so we celebrated with them our special day, our eightieth year, our birthdays.
The first day of December was a day I will never forget. The children threw us both a wonderful birthday ball. It was at Jonas', everything was beautifully decorated, the food delicious and tasteful, and all of our relatives and friends were there. We both liked that very much and I will never forget that lovely time, and we will remain grateful to our children for all of their work and wonderful welcome.

How quickly these years pass. When you realize that old age is already here, though we don't feel that we are old, but the years do what the years will do.
When I think sometimes about the years that have passed by, I think that they were not bad to us, though there were many that oppressed the heart. We were the most sad for our daughter when, after twenty-nine years of marriage, her husband left and no longer wanted to be married to her. There was so much she had to live through, that after so many years she was left alone. And the two of us suffered a great deal of pain seeing that, and we were very sad for her and for her sons, who had to live through that, too. Though it was very hard, all is now going well. Ramutė is living happily now. Biliukas has

his own family, his own clinic, has a good practice, is building a very beautiful home, and his daughters are very good and pleasant girls. He has a beautiful and good wife who helps him a great deal. Their life is going well. Davukas also has a good job in the hospital, as a children's doctor.

We are so fortunate with our children and grandchildren, because all of them look at life seriously. We rejoice with our grandchildren, they are beautiful, and good to us.

All of our grandchildren are good and well, so what more could we want. Only to rejoice and to ask God that they will all be healthy and happy.

2013

We have finally reached the thirteenth year. The twelfth year was not so good to us. In April, my last brother died. He was the oldest of us. I remain alone and the last of my family. I suppose it's destined that some one needs to be the last.

We have reached the sixty-fifth year of our life together. But I don't see how anything has changed. Life moves ahead. We now rejoice in each day.

The children are good, the grandchildren are good, everyone gets along well, they come to visit us, so we are so fortunate with our family.

We have celebrated our eighty-fifth year. We feel pretty well.

The thirteenth year has come and we will see what it brings us.

Now, on February 5, we are flying to Florida for a month. My daughter has given us a great gift. It will be wonderful to spend time with her.

This is where Janina's letter to her family ends. She went on to live for almost six more years, during that time telling the stories of her life, quietly and lovingly, to her children and grandchildren and great-grandchildren. Those years were highlighted by many joyful gatherings and celebrations, by delicious meals and so much laughter, though they were marked as well by the losses of family and friends, including her beloved Alfonsas, who died at home on December 30, 2016, cared for by Janina. They had been together for more than seventy-one years. She died on October 9, 2018, after a short illness and two months before her 91st birthday. She is buried next to Alfonsas in Cedar Hill Cemetery in a quiet spot under the trees. Her youngest son, Algirdas, died a little more than five weeks after she died and is buried with his parents.

JANINA DRESLIUS ZDANYS

Janina Zdanys died peacefully on October 9, 2018, cared for by her children and grandchildren, whom she loved deeply and whose lives she celebrated each day with joy. She was born on December 9, 1927, in Kaunas, Lithuania, daughter of the late Arturas and Viktorija (Župerkaitė) Dreslius. During the Second World War, she and her family escaped the Russian occupation of Lithuania and lived for nearly five years in a refugee camp in Seligenstadt, Germany, under the sponsorship of the United Nations Relief and Rehabilitation Administration. It was there that she met her husband Alfonsas, to whom she was married for seventy years. They came to the United States in August 1949, settling first in Vermont as part of a U.S. Department of Agriculture refugee resettlement program, and in 1950 moved to New Britain, where she raised her children and worked in local manufacturing. In 1969, she and Alfonsas bought the Maple Motel in Newington, which they owned and operated until retiring in 1985. Those years were a special fulfillment of the interests she had as a young girl in the challenges and rewards of running her own business.

    Janina was predeceased by her husband, by her parents, and by her brothers Pranas, Povilas, and Stasys. She leaves her children, Ramutė Mills of Brecksville, OH, and Gintaras Karosas; Jonas and Jean Zdanys of Wallingford; Leonas and Mary Ellen Zdanys of Woodstock; and Algirdas Zdanys of Newington, who resided with her. She also leaves six grandchildren, for whom she will always be their beloved Grammy and their favorite cook: William and Renee Mills of Chagrin Falls, OH; David Mills and Molly Jones of Mt. Pleasant, SC; Kristina Zdanys and Algis Kalvaitis of West Hartford; Joanna Zdanys and Jason Lee of Brooklyn, NY; Lee Zdanys of Woodstock; and Jessica Zdanys of Waterford. And, she leaves seven greatgrand-children: Alexa, Kate, and Anna Mills of Chagrin Falls; Laura and Julia Kalvaitis of West Hartford; and Nora and Ben Zdanys of Woodstock.

ALFONSAS ZDANYS

Alfonsas Zdanys died peacefully in his home in Newington on December 30, cared for by his wife and children. He was born on November 5, 1927, in Kybartai, Lithuania, son of the late Juozas and Stefanija (Skimbirauskaitė) Zdancevičius. A gifted and enthusiastic storyteller, he talked often about his life in that small town. He talked also about the difficulties he faced after the Russian occupation of Lithuania and how he and his family spent three months walking from Lithuania to the West, caught between the German and Russian armies as the Second World War came to its conclusion. That long walk ended in a refugee camp in Seligenstadt, Germany, sponsored by the United Nations Relief and Rehabilitation Administration, where Alfonsas lived for nearly five years, serving in the camp's police force and participating in athletic and cultural activities. It was there that he met and married his wife, Janina (Dreslius), to whom he was married for seventy years. They came to the United States in August 1949, settling first in Vermont as part of a U.S. Department of Agriculture refugee resettlement program, and in 1950 moved to New Britain, where he worked in local manufacturing. In 1969, they bought the Maple Motel in Newington, which they owned and operated until retiring in 1985. During those years he was also active in the choirs of St. Andrew's Church in New Britain and Holy Trinity Church in Hartford. That led to the creation of a men's quartet and later trio that toured Lithuanian communities throughout the Northeast performing traditional and modern Lithuanian music. Those years were highlights of a vigorous lifelong commitment to singing. All who knew Alfonsas marveled at the joy he felt when lifting his voice and telling his story through song.

Alfonsas leaves his wife Janina; his children Ramutė Mills of Brecksville, OH, and Gintaras Karosas; Jonas and Jean Zdanys of Wallingford; Leonas and Mary Ellen Zdanys of Woodstock; and Algirdas Zdanys of Newington. He also leaves six grandchildren: William and Renee Mills of Chagrin Falls, OH; David Mills and Molly Jones of Mt. Pleasant, SC; Kristina Zdanys and Algis Kalvaitis of West Hartford; Joanna Zdanys and Jason Lee of Brooklyn, NY; Lee Zdanys of Woodstock; and Jessica Zdanys of Waterford. And, he leaves six great-grandchildren: Alexa, Kate, and Anna Mills of Chagrin Falls; Laura Kalvaitis of West Hartford; and Nora and Ben Zdanys of Woodstock. He was predeceased by his parents and by his sisters and brothers Eugenija, Ona (Ditrichas), Algimantas, Vitas, and Jonas.

www.ingramcontent.com/pod-product-compliance
Lightning Source LLC
Chambersburg PA
CBHW061232070526
44584CB00030B/4089